A Young Vic production

Sting

by Sophie Swithinbank

Sting was first performed at the Young Vic Theatre, London, on 18 June 2026.

STING

by Sophie Swithinbank
Directed by Nancy Medina

CAST

Dom	Nick Blood
Lily	Phoebe Ladenburg
Ash	Adelle Leonce

CREATIVE TEAM

Writer	Sophie Swithinbank
Director	Nancy Medina
Designer	Debbie Duru
Lighting Designer	Ryan Day
Composer & Sound Designer	Nicola T. Chang
Movement Director	Rachael Nanyonjo
Casting Director	Lisa Makin
Fight and Intimacy Director	Yarit Dor
Production Dramatherapist	Samantha Adams
Voice Coach	Carol Fairlamb
Costume Supervisor	Aimee Russam
Jerwood Assistant Director	Olivia Millar-Ross
Linbury Design Associate	Yi Gao
Genesis Design Assistant	Gisela Mulindwa

PRODUCTION & STAGE MANAGEMENT TEAM

Production Manager	Carmel Macaree
Stage Manager	Martha Mamo
Deputy Stage Manager	Catriona McHugh

Developed with Lidless Theatre Company. Inspired by concepts from Waking the Witch, developed in 2022 with Sophie Swithinbank, Lisa Lapidge and Jess Tucker Boyd.

Olwyn FOUNDATION *for* WOMEN AND GIRLS

About the Young Vic

Founded in 1970 as a space for world-premiere productions and unexpected takes on classic plays, the Young Vic has been one of London's leading theatres for more than fifty years.

Welcoming 100,000 visitors a year, the Young Vic stands out in the nation's cultural landscape for balancing daring commercial drive and artistic flair with genuine grassroots social impact work within our community. This success is seen most vividly in the audience group for which we are famous; the most diverse, lively and engaged in London. This is the fruit of years of building involvement among local young people. We forge deep connections in our neighbourhood through our Taking Part programme, where we engage with over 15,000 people every year via a wide range of projects, from skills-based workshops to on-stage performances.

We believe great art belongs to everyone. Ticket prices are kept low no matter how high the demand and 10% of tickets are given free within the local community; enabling a unique, no-risk taste of great theatre for thousands of people.

Our unique, fully-flexible auditoria allows us to present great plays by and with the next generation of theatre artists alongside work by some of the world's great directors, actors and designers. We are proud to be a Director's Theatre known for launching careers and a combination of youth and genius which makes us one of the most vibrant theatres in the UK.

Built upon the principles of access, innovation, and community, the Young Vic is deepening its roots nationally and internationally. Recent transfers include *Punch*, *Best of Enemies* and *Oklahoma!* in the West End and *Death of a Salesman* and *The Collaboration* on Broadway.

Some theatres present great plays. Some give young artists opportunities to grow. Some build strong and lasting relationships with their community. The Young Vic does all three.

Artistic Director	Nadia Fall OBE
Executive Director	Lucy Pattison

youngvic.org

Supported using public funding by ARTS COUNCIL ENGLAND
Southwark Council
Lambeth

STING

Sophie Swithinbank

Acknowledgements

I would like to thank Jess Tucker Boyd, Lisa Lapidge and the team at the Au Brana Creative Residency, for igniting the furious, curious spark what would eventually become *Sting*.

Thank you to Max Harrison for encouraging me to re-work an early draft of *Sting*, after I had rejected it as a 'bad idea' and buried it in a drawer for two years. I would like to thank Zoe Weldon at Lidless Theatre for funding and supporting an eye-opening R&D, directed by Max Harrison and featuring stunning performances by Nadia Parks, Adeline Waby and Alessandro Piavani. I would like to thank Sarah-Jane Ewart (SJ), a barrister who works closely with the Centre for Women's Justice and specialises in cases of police perpetrated domestic abuse, for giving up her time to share her valuable insights with us.

Thank you to Jack Bradley for sending the play to Lisa Makin and Lisa Makin for sending the play to Nadia Fall, and Nadia Fall for programming it. Sean Brookes, our incredible producer. Mark Starling, my agent, my constant guide and cheerleader. Bridget and Chris Swithinbank, for their endless love and support. And Ben Target, who tells me every day that he is proud of me. I couldn't have done any of this without you.

I would especially like to thank all the women whose stories feature in *Sting*, many of whom are no longer with us. I hope you, and your stories, can live on through this play.

S.S.

‘Figures obtained through freedom of information requests from 41 forces across the UK show that more than 1300 police officers and staff have been reported for alleged domestic abuse since 2018. Only 36 have been dismissed.’

Sarah Haque, *The Bureau of Investigative Journalism*, 2022

Characters

ASH
LILY
DOM
OFFICER (*played by Ash*)
PANTALAIMON, *a rabbit*

Notes

A slash (/) indicates an interruption.

A comma (,) on a separate line indicates a beat.

An en dash (–) at the end of a line indicates an unfinished thought.

An en dash (–) on a separate line indicates a pregnant pause.

Words in (brackets) are implied not spoken.

Design

Archive. Hive. Small things hiding inside bigger things.

This text went to press before the end of rehearsals and so may differ slightly from the play as performed.

ACT ONE

Club

ASH *dances alone, fecklessly, a rite towards death.*

As she dances, invisible people rip her apart, painful and pleasurable.

As the music reaches a climax –

– something magical happens, a split in time, and suddenly…

Archive

ASH *is at work, sweaty, breathless, inappropriately dressed.*

LILY. Um. Hello?

ASH *gets her phone out and looks at it.*

Can I help you?

ASH. Sorry, no, hi, sorry. I was just checking the address. I'm. Am I? Is this…? (*Reading from her phone.*) Howard Hall Ar-chive (*Pronounced 'chive'.*)?

LILY. Archive. Yeah.

ASH. I'm starting here today.

LILY. You're the archive assistant?

ASH. Yes.

LILY *senses there is something wrong with* ASH.

LILY. Where did you / come from?

ASH. My supervisor forwarded me / the job listing.

LILY. No I mean, why are you dressed like that?

ASH *looks down, takes in the differences in how they are dressed:*

ASH *is wearing a see-through mesh top, tight shorts, a cropped jacket, trainers. Her clothes have a grubby, sweaty, end-of-the-night feel.* LILY *is wearing loose, sensible clothing, her glasses on a string round her neck. She is wearing knitted slippers with a pom-pom on the toe.*

ASH. What's going on with those pom-pom shoes?

LILY. These are my work slippers. I don't wear outdoor shoes in here.

ASH *looks down at her dirty trainers, slips them off.*

ASH. I've got my… contract email thing.

ASH *shows* LILY *an email on her phone.*

I'm working for… Lily Holmes.

LILY. I'm Lily.

ASH (*pretending to be pleased*). Great. Lovely. I'm Ash. Aisling.

They have reached an impasse.

I'm really looking forward to, um, getting to know the library and –

LILY. It's an archive.

ASH. A hive of words and information. Like a library.

LILY. Well yes. But in a library, things are replaceable. In an archive –

ASH. These are the originals.

LILY. Yes.

I was um, they told me. I was expecting one of the post-doc students.

ASH. Oh, yeah I am.

LILY. You are what.

ASH. I've just finished my PhD. Criminal Justice and Social Policy.

,

LILY. How come you didn't know how to pronounce archive?

ASH. I was just being… I like playing with words. Archive. Hive. Chive. Arch.

Small words hiding inside bigger words.

LILY. Well it just, gave me the wrong impression of you.

ASH. I know. I like testing how quick people are to judge.

LILY *does an awkward laugh,* ASH *joins in the laugh.*

You were quite quick.

LILY. Um, well. Sorry.

I didn't realise I was being tested.

,

I have a desk for you over / here –

ASH (*gasps*). I love it. I'm gonna get a fern. For oxygen.

LILY. You can't have a fern. This is a temperature-controlled environment.

ASH. Maybe a scented candle then?

LILY. A candle?

ASH. For atmosphere.

,

LILY. Have you worked in an archive before?

ASH. Yes.

I guess just. Different archives, different rules.

LILY. I don't know any archive that would allow you to have a naked flame, but anyway. Okay. It's a part-time position. Mondays, Wednesdays, Thursdays. The bulk of the job is creating a digital catalogue for all the different accusations of witchcraft from the late sixteen-hundreds to the early seventeen-hundreds. Are you familiar with archival cataloguing standards?

ASH. Yes.

LILY. I use ISAD.

ASH. Yes.

LILY. So we're largely cataloguing accusations that involved the death of livestock, accusations that involved sexual activity, and –

ASH. Marks on the body?

LILY. Yeah.

ASH. Seizures?

LILY. Right.

ASH. Death of infants?

LILY. Yes. And some of that material is quite upsetting so –

ASH. It's okay. I'm fine.

LILY. I'm working towards figuring out how much has really changed. I'm writing a book about victim blaming from the seventeenth century, to today. About how the justice system is built on misogyny and therefore can't ever really work for women.

ASH. That's um…

LILY. I know it's a bit niche. But when I began working in this section of the archive, it just. It was all blindingly obvious somehow and I pitched the / idea to –

ASH. No I was going to say, that sounds amazing. The book.

LILY. Oh right.

,

Thanks.

Well. Anyway – we have over three hundred original articles in this section of the archive. And the catalogue we're building will mean they can be understood in a modern context and compared – (ASH *is moving towards a file containing original documents.*) with how the justice system operates today.

ASH. Should I wear gloves? To handle these?

LILY. No. You only need the gloves to handle photographs – (*Making herself laugh.*) and we're not likely to come across any of those.

ASH *doesn't get the joke.*

Because there were no cameras in the seventeenth century.

ASH *fake-laughs.*

She takes off her jacket, hanging it on the back of her desk chair.

LILY *averts her gaze.*

Oh my god sorry.

ASH. What?

LILY. That.

A mark on ASH*'s neck: a love bite.*

ASH (*laughing*). Oh fuck. Sorry.

I forgot that was there.

She sees a scarf hanging on a peg and puts it on.

LILY. That's my scarf.

ASH. Oh. Can I borrow it?

She's already wearing it.

LILY. It's like someone's tried to to to eat you.

ASH. Maybe they have.

LILY. Who?

ASH. Nosy.

LILY. Sorry, I /

ASH. We've only just met.

’

LILY. Look. You… you've obviously… had a big night out, or something.

ASH (*laughing*). 'Big Night Out.'

LILY. And I just think. Maybe you should pop home, put some clothes on, have a shower, come back.

ASH. You serious?

LILY. Yes.

ASH. Will I still get paid?

LILY. You'll get paid for the amount of time you're here.

ASH. But I'm here now.

LILY. Think you just need to sort yourself out a bit and / then

ASH. Sort myself out?

LILY. Yeah. Yes. If that's okay –

ASH. Who's going to do your catalogue?

Who's going to tidy up the library?

LILY. Archive.

ASH. But you're lonely.

LILY. Pardon?

ASH. Isn't that why you asked for an assistant?

LILY. No, it's just. It's a lot of work and…

ASH *sits down at her desk, typing into her computer, clicking the mouse.*

What are you doing?

ASH *continues typing, clicking.*

You don't have a login yet.

ASH *continues typing, clicking.*

You're just typing into the screensaver.

ASH *continues typing, clicking.*

ASH. I've made a password.

LILY. How?

ASH. It's Ash underscore Computer underscore one.

LILY. Don't tell me your password.

ASH. Oh. Sorry.

Shall I change it?

LILY. Let's just get started. (*Leaning over* ASH*'s shoulder.*) So if you just open this folder. All the catalogues are in there.

ASH *has a pain in her lower abdomen.*

And then if you go to Excel…

ASH*'s pain increases.*

Are you okay with Excel?

ASH. Yeah. Yep, fine.

Without either of them touching it, the radio turns on.

LILY *turns the radio off, unnerved.*

ASH*'s pain increases.*

LILY. So there's a different page of the spreadsheet for each…

LILY *looks down at* ASH*'s lap.*

Oh. You're bleeding.

ASH *looks down.*

Blood seeps through her shorts, down the inside of her legs.

Frozen for a moment, they both just silently watch the blood spread.

ASH. Fuck. Sorry.

ASH *falls to the floor.*

LILY. It's okay. You're okay.

ASH. What's happening?

LILY. I don't know… is there any chance…

ASH *cries out.*

Is there any chance you might be pregnant?

ASH *cries out again.*

You might be having a miscarriage.

ASH. Why? What?!

LILY. You're going to be okay.

Just lean on me. That's it. There's a shower through here.

ASH *and* LILY *are shadows behind frosted glass.*

The shower turns on.

The lights flicker.

The radio again, but heavy static/white noise: a male voice listing women's names (*Bridget Bishop, Sarah Good, Wilmot Redd, Salem*) *but we can't make out the sounds.*

DOM *walks through, carrying a cardboard box. He stops, notices the shower, the shadows moving behind the frosted glass, he moves on.*

LILY *comes out of the shower. She cleans the blood off her hands. She dithers, not knowing what to do next.*

(*To no one.*) Kettle on.

She puts the kettle on.

She finds some spare clothes in her cupboard, slides them through the bathroom door.

There's some clean clothes here and I've got the kettle on and –

The shower stops.

No movement.

ASH *comes out in* LILY*'s clothes.*

Wow. That was quick.

ASH *sits in* LILY*'s clothes, altered.*

LILY *makes the tea.*

(*Handing the tea to* ASH.) It's ginger and turmeric.

ASH *takes the tea.*

ASH. (Thank you.)

,

LILY. Do you want a bag? For your clothes?

,

I'll pop them in a bag.

She puts the bloodied clothes into a bag.

Should we um… do you need a lift anywhere?

,

Aisling?

ASH. Sorry.

LILY. Do you need a lift somewhere?

ASH. No thanks. My boyfriend's coming.

LILY. Oh that's good. Great.

Now?

ASH. Yeah.

LILY. Good. Much nicer to be together. Is he taking you straight to the hospital or –

ASH. Home.

LILY. Right. Yes.

You should go to the hospital soon though. Because sometimes they have to (suction)…

,

Well. Quite a mad first day, isn't it?

LILY *finds herself laughing. So does* ASH *– the ridiculousness of it.*

Normally it's just. Setting up your login and your pass key and…

DOM *comes through the door, sombre, worried. A moment of confusion.*

DOM. I thought you were having (an emergency)… Why are you laughing?

ASH. No, it's just… I don't know

ASH*'s laughter turns to crying.*

He walks over to her.

LILY. Sorry – your shoes.

He stops.

DOM. What?

LILY. Nothing. Never mind.

He continues over to ASH*, who dissolves into tears in his arms.*

DOM. It's okay, it's okay.

LILY *feels slightly awkward witnessing such an intimate moment. She tidies her desk (which is already immaculate).*

ASH *and* DOM *finally break their embrace.*

DOM. We're going to be okay.

Come on. Let's get in the car.

ASH (*to* LILY). Thanks. For – yeah.

ASH *leaves.*

DOM *starts to follow.*

LILY. Hi, sorry. (*Holding out the bag of clothes.*) This is… Aisling's clothes.

DOM (*taking the bag*). Oh right, thanks. Sorry I'm… (in shock)

LILY. No no, of course. Don't apologise. Please. She's wearing my clothes, but no rush with that. Honestly. I've got loads of. Other clothes.

DOM. That's really kind. Thank you. I'll get them washed / and return them

LILY. Honestly, / no worries.

DOM. I'm really glad someone was with her.

LILY. Absolutely.

DOM. I mean. It should have been me. With her.

LILY. Of course. Horrible. To not be together for… yeah.

From outside, ASH *beeps the car horn.*

I should let you go.

DOM. Yeah. She can take a few days off I'm guessing?

LILY. Of course. Yes.

DOM. Thanks Lily. And yeah, thanks for…

LILY. Oh yeah no…

Sorry.

DOM. What?

LILY. No, nothing. I just… did I tell you my name?

DOM. Oh, no. Ash was texting me.

LILY. Right.

DOM. Right.

Thanks again.

Familiar

Back at the flat, ASH *and* DOM, *motionless silence.* ASH *is wrapped in a blanket. The bag of clothes sits on the table between them.*

DOM. Shall I put these in the wash?

,

Ash?

,

I'm going to put them in the wash.

He exits, puts the wash on, comes back, sits opposite ASH.

ASH. Was it okay, to leave work early?

DOM. Trent came in, he'll do a double shift.

ASH. That's nice of him.

DOM. Yeah.

,

Hey, I got you a present.

ASH (*smiling, despite herself, sitting up from her burrito blanket*). What?

DOM *gets the cardboard box and carefully puts it on the table.*

What is it?

DOM. Open it. Careful.

She opens the box. Surrounded by straw: a little bunny rabbit.

She gasps.

ASH. Whaaaaaaat the hell.

She picks up the bunny.

DOM. I was at the shelter today, and this new family arrived and they weren't allowed to bring the rabbit in, and the little girl was crying, and refusing to go inside and it was pissing it down, so I said

I know someone who can look after him.

ASH. ME!

DOM (*laughing*). Yeah.

ASH. I love him.

DOM. So you want to keep him then?

ASH. Yes!

DOM. Okay, you have to look after him though. Cleaning, feeding, all that.

ASH. Yeah yeah, I will.

DOM. Otherwise I'll just take him to Pets at Home.

ASH. I'll do all of it.

What's his name?

DOM. I think the little girl said Pam? Or maybe Pan? Like Peter Pan?

ASH. Pan like Pantalaimon?

DOM. Like what?

ASH. You know, the dæmon.

DOM. What demon?

ASH. From the the the book.

DOM. Okay.

ASH. This is the best day of my life.

DOM *laughs.*

What? I love him. This is love.

DOM. Yeah, you did also have a miscarriage today though.

ASH. –

DOM. It's just weird to say it's the best day of your life.

ASH. I can feel lots of different things at once.

DOM. Ash.

ASH. Yeah no I can see how that is weird, yes.

DOM. Shall we talk about it?

ASH *cuddles Pan.*

I think it would be good to talk about it.

DOM *gently takes Pan and puts him in the box.*

ASH. There's not really anything to say.

DOM. Why didn't you tell me?

ASH. Tell you what?

DOM. That you were pregnant.

ASH. I didn't know.

If I'd known I wouldn't have been out getting wasted.

DOM. You were wasted?

ASH. No. Just you know. Out. Not like wasted but…

DOM *puts his head in his hands.*

We're not actually grieving. Are we?

Are you sad about it?

DOM. Yes.

ASH. Are you?

DOM. Of course I'm sad about it.

ASH. Oh. Sorry.

She goes to him and hugs him.

DOM (*in the hug*). I think I would have really liked to do that with you.

ASH *comes out of the hug.*

ASH. Yeah?

DOM. Yeah.

They kiss.

He notices the love bite.

What's that?

ASH (*smiling*). What do you mean?

DOM. What is it?

ASH. You did that.

DOM. When?

ASH. The other night.

DOM. Did I?

ASH. Yeah.

A tangled beat, tense.

DOM (*laughing*). Oh my god, yeah. I did!

They both laugh.

ASH. You're a succubus.

Playfully he leans in, to give her another one. She squeals.

(*Mock.*) Noo! Save me from the succubus!

Their faces are close together.

DOM. Maybe we should think about it.

ASH. What?

DOM. A baby.

ASH. Dom, I'm pretty much still bleeding.

DOM. Ash.

ASH. I can't think about a baby right now.

DOM. No, yeah – sorry.

ASH. Also I've only just moved in. We don't need to rush.

DOM. No you haven't.

ASH. What?

DOM. You haven't just moved in.

It's been like – almost five months.

An impasse.

You could at least finish unpacking.

ASH. I just haven't got round to it.

DOM. Because you keep going out and getting wasted.

,

,

I'm just.

Maybe I am grieving, or something.

He starts cleaning the kitchen forensically, spraying and wiping.

Going on the break was really hard for me. That's just. That's all I'm saying.

ASH. It was your idea.

DOM. It was not my idea.

ASH. You said you couldn't be around me.

,

But I wanted to come back. To you.

DOM. Okay. So be here.

ASH. I love you.

DOM. Really be here.

She kisses him.

ASH. I am here.

He believes her.

DOM. Good.

A confirming kiss. ASH *comes out of the kiss with a new thought:*

ASH. I'll take a little present for Lily tomorrow.

DOM. What?

ASH. To say thanks.

DOM. Well, no, you don't have to go to work tomorrow, babe.

ASH. Why?

DOM. You need time off. To rest.

ASH. I'm fine.

DOM. You're not fine, Ash. I asked her, she said you can take a few days.

I'm going to look after you.

Executions

A few days later, LILY *is in the archive, labelling boxes, listening to the radio.*

News on radio: '…her report identified major red flags that were missed and repeatedly ignored during various instances / of –'

LILY *hears a noise, someone moving around in the back room.*

LILY. Hello?

Another noise – maybe something breaking.

She grabs a staple gun as a weapon.

ASH *stumbles in, covered in ash.*

The news moves onto a different headline, about a woman who was doused in petrol and burned alive in her home (but we don't hear it properly due to the following confrontation):

LILY *fires the staple gun.*

They both scream.

The staple narrowly misses ASH.

ASH. Fucking hell.

ASH *turns the radio off.*

LILY *is still screaming.*

You nearly stapled me!

LILY. I didn't know you were here.

ASH. Well I am here.

LILY. How did you get in?

ASH. How did you not see me coming in?

LILY. You didn't say you were coming back today.

ASH. I did.

,

LILY. What's on your clothes?

ASH. Dust? LILY. Ash?

ASH. What?

LILY. No I mean, is it ash?

,

Did you sleep here? In the back.

ASH. Why would I sleep here?

LILY. I don't know.

ASH. Did *you* sleep here?

LILY. What?

ASH. Is that why you're so early?

LILY. This is my normal time.

ASH. Do you want me to sleep here?

LILY. Pardon?

ASH. Rather than going home.

LILY. Why would I want you to sleep here?

ASH *shrugs.*

Look, we obviously got off to a bit of an unusual start. With the…

ASH. Did it stain? The blood?

LILY. No no.

Well it did, but I scrubbed it. Felt like I was covering up a murder (!)

Not funny.

So yeah. Bit of a mad start but I'm…

I'm glad you're here, actually. Because I need to update you on something that might alter our schedule a bit.

ASH. Go on.

LILY. I'm helping with a police investigation.

ASH. Really? Why?

LILY. I can't say. I have to sign a non-disclosure…

But, well… there's been these three deaths recently. Three women. They're investigating whether the deaths could be connected.

ASH (*sotto*). Oh fuck, like a serial killer?

LILY. Well, no one's saying those words –

ASH. Yet.

LILY. Well yeah.

ASH. Carmella Riccardo, Sara Ustinov and Taylor Jackson?

The radio comes on, a bad-signal voice whispers, 'Agnes Waterhouse, Violet Mar–'

I think something's wrong with the radio.

LILY. I know. I need to fix it.

LILY *turns the radio off.*

The coroners have released some information for the investigation.

ASH. What information?

LILY. The causes of death, all look like… in the style of… executions.

Carmella was burned alive.

Sara was hanged.

Taylor drowned.

There might be patterns. Ritualistic patterns. Across the cases. Replications of historical / witch executions.

ASH. Witch executions.

The last woman in the UK burned alive as a form of execution was Catherine Hayes in 1726.

LILY. Yeah, but maybe it wasn't.

ASH. Maybe it was last week.

'

Why have they come to you? The police.

LILY. Because. I'm a historical expert on the topic.

ASH. Right. So I'm like… the deputy expert.

LILY. Sure, if you like.

,

ASH. Taylor Jackson's dog attacked a nine-year-old boy.

LILY. What?

ASH. That's one of the deeds of witches. Conducting animals to attack.

LILY. Was the boy killed?

ASH. Calling familiars to undertake evil deeds.

The boy survived, the dog was euthanised, Taylor got six months.

,

LILY. Maybe you're the expert.

ASH. Maybe.

,

LILY. Why did you sleep here?

ASH. I didn't.

LILY. How did you get in then?

ASH. I borrowed the spare pass.

She produces the spare pass from her pocket.

Got in early, did some repairs on the Agnes Godfrey court records.

LILY (*panicked*). What?

ASH. You know that woman who was accused of drowning that horse. And the pig and piglet.

LILY. No, I know, but what repairs did you do?

ASH. The parchment was decaying. I just reinforced it.

LILY. You reinforced the parchment?

ASH. Yes.

LILY. Did you use the soft brush?

ASH. Yes.

LILY. Did you use the acid-free tracing paper?

ASH. Yes! Jesus.

And then I transcribed it for the digital catalogue, in the death of livestock section.

LILY. You transcribed it?

ASH. Yes.

LILY. It's from 1598.

ASH. I know.

LILY. It's in Latin.

ASH. I know it's in Latin. I transcribed it to English.

,

Tea?

She goes to make the tea.

Kettle boiling.

,

LILY (*seeing* ASH *in a bright new light*). Do you want to go for a drink tonight?

ASH *looks up, mischief brewing.*

ASH. A drink, you say?

LILY. I was planning on a sort of 'welcome drink' on your first day, but you know…

My advance just came through, for the book.

So drinks on me! If you want.

Just a soft drink, if you're still feeling a bit… (*Vaguely gesturing to her abdomen.*)

ASH. Yeah alright. That sounds nice.

Kettle boils.

Welcome Drink

In the pub.

LILY *raises her glass.*

LILY. Welcome to my team. Of one (!)

ASH. Well, two now.

They clink. Sip their drinks.

Neither of them have anything else to say…

ASH *looks around the pub.*

LILY. So um, Dom seems nice.

How did you two meet?

ASH. Uummm…

LILY. Was it an app? It's always the apps now isn't it?

ASH. We met in real life actually.

,

Is she going to expand on this?

LILY. Where?

ASH. Well it was… it was just one of those moments, you know?

LILY. What moments?

ASH. Where you meet someone and it just feels big. Significant.

LILY. I don't really…

ASH. It sort of hits you in the face and says, 'hello, I'm here!'

LILY. Love at first sight, I guess. Is what people call it.

ASH. Yeah. That.

They sip their drinks.

He gave me his number. And he said call any time. And I did.

And, I'll be honest – he was just. Amazing. He just, changed me. Pulled me up. Like a rope out of a well.

LILY. A well?

ASH. Yeah, because I was a bit stuck. In a… bad situation. With someone. And Dom helped me… (out.)

,

LILY. Well. Sounds like you met the right person at the right time.

ASH. Yeah.

How about / you?

LILY. But you know, actually, the thing with that is, it still requires you being able to climb a rope.

ASH. What?

LILY. I mean. Dom threw you a rope, which is amazing, he's obviously brilliant – but you still had to climb up it.

ASH. Mmm.

LILY. I'm just saying, give yourself some credit too. Not all heroes wear capes.

ASH. He doesn't wear a cape.

LILY. No you, I mean. You got yourself out of the…

Those things are hard to get out of.

ASH *looks at* LILY, *curious.*

What?

ASH. You know.

LILY. I do know.

They settle in to knowing each other slightly better.

,

,

How long have you been together?

ASH. Nearly a year.

LILY. Oh! So it's quite new then?

ASH (*shrugs*). Doesn't feel new. Feels like I've known him for hundreds of years.

(*Laughing.*) I had a dream last night that I proposed to him by putting a ring inside some raw mincemeat and then he cooked the mince to make a bolognese, and found the ring.

LILY*'s face is saying 'ergh'.*

What?

LILY. Was it not quite greasy?

ASH. No. It was perfect.

,

LILY. So is that? A plan you intend to action?

ASH. What?

LILY. This… mincemeat proposal?

ASH. Oh no no fuck no.

He's actually already married.

LILY. Oh!

ASH. Well, no, he's been married. He's separated. But they have a daughter together so…

LILY. Right.

ASH. He sees her as much as possible. His daughter.

She's so cute. I haven't actually met her. But in pictures. She's gorgeous.

LILY *smiles, sips her drink.*

,

LILY. Hiding things in food actually used to be considered as an unleashing of the occult. In Salem one of the things they did to test if a woman was a witch was to mix her urine into a cake and then feed the cake to the family dog and then if the dog became attracted to the woman it meant she was having dark communications with animals and was, therefore, a 'witch'.

LILY *U-turns to more normal small-talk.*

So where did you grow up?

ASH. Sheffield. You?

LILY. Oh, we moved around a lot.

ASH. Who's we?

LILY. Me and, um, lots of other people. A big community of.

Well it was a cult actually. I grew up in a cult.

ASH. Oh right.

LILY. Yeah. (It was quite bad.)

My parents are still in it. My dad's quite a high-ranking elder now so he's got several wives and –

ASH. Wow. Okay.

,

And you?

LILY. What?

ASH. How many wives do you have?

LILY *does a sharp honking laugh.*

LILY. Oh. None. No. I Don't.

ASH. You never know.

LILY. Well no, I do know.

ASH. You never know what could be waiting round the corner. The love of your life could be in this pub.

LILY *looks at* ASH. ASH *looks around the pub.*

LILY. This is my local. If the love of my life was here, I would have met them already.

,

ASH. Well maybe we should go looking elsewhere.

LILY. What do you mean?

ASH. Do you want to go out?

LILY. We are out.

ASH. We could go out-out. Celebrate your book advance.

LILY. This is enough out for me, thanks.

ASH. Let's go clubbing.

LILY. Absolutely no way. Not. No.

ASH. Why not?

LILY. This is about as out as I go, thank you.

A sudden cut to the club.

Loud music. Strobe lights and laser beams make it difficult to make out what is happening.

They get closer together.

They dance.

ASH *puts her hand on* LILY*'s face and whispers into her ear… or was it a kiss? It's hard to see, in the strobe light, but then –*

DOM *turns on the lights and* ASH *lands…*

Late

...back at the flat, out of breath and sweaty.

DOM *is in his pyjamas.*

ASH. Hi.

DOM. It's three in the morning.

ASH. Sorry.

Went for a drink.

She goes to Pan's hutch, which is concealed in the wall.

She opens it, picks him up, kisses and cuddles him.

DOM. Who did you go with?

ASH. Lily. To welcome me to the team.

Went to The Level.

DOM. The Level? You've barely met her and you're going clubbing?

ASH (*shrugs*). She's not like, going to be my best mate, but –

I like her. She's really interesting.

DOM. Is she?

ASH. She grew up in a cult.

DOM. I bet she did.

ASH. What does that mean?

DOM. She's quite strange. Is what that means.

ASH *heads to the bathroom.*

ASH. You met her for about ten seconds....

DOM. Is she gay?

ASH. What?

DOM. Is she a lesbian?

ASH. I don't know. Maybe.

I'm not just going to randomly ask her if she's gay.

DOM. You can't ask people anything these days.

ASH (*makes a face*). That makes you sound very old. When you say things like that.

DOM *hides his anger by tidying some crumbs into the bin.*

DOM. Is it quite busy at work then?

ASH. What do you mean?

DOM. Coz you also left super early this morning.

ASH. Did I?

DOM. You'd already gone when I got home from the night shift.

ASH. How was the night shift?

DOM. Where did you go?

ASH. When?

DOM. This morning.

ASH. –

DOM. I just. I'm just trying to look out for you.

ASH. Well I don't need you to do that. Anymore.

DOM. –

ASH. What?!

DOM. I need to ask you something.

ASH. Okay.

ASH *puts Pan back into his hutch.*

DOM. Was it mine?

The baby.

ASH. Well that's a stupid fucking question.

DOM. Is it?

ASH. Of course it was yours.

DOM. You didn't… sleep with anyone…

ASH. No!

DOM. …while we were on that break?

She doesn't speak, but from her body language it's obvious that she did.

Ash.

ASH. We used protection.

DOM. With who?

ASH. Why does it matter?

DOM. Who was it?

ASH. We were on a break, Dom!

DOM. Well whoever the fuck it was, got you fucking pregnant!

He didn't mean to raise his voice.

ASH. You're scaring Pantalaimon.

DOM. And then, clearly you went out and got wasted on purpose to get rid of it, so that I'd never know.

ASH. Sorry, have you gone mad?

DOM. If I go through the bins, will I find a pregnancy test?

ASH. If you go through the bins?

DOM. Yeah.

ASH. Babe, please don't go through the bins.

DOM. Why?

ASH. Because that's disgusting.

DOM. Was it Charlie? Charlie's?

ASH. What?

DOM. Was it Charlie? During the break.

ASH. (Possibly.) No.

It was not fucking Charlie, for fuck's sake.

Why are you being like this?

DOM. Why do you keep going out and not telling me where you are?

,

Do you not *want* to be here with me?

ASH. Not right now, no.

Because you're being a cunt.

Danger in the air.

DOM *goes over to the door and locks it.*

What are you doing?

DOM. Locking the door.

ASH. Why?

,

DOM. Because you left it unlocked.

,

Are you planning to do a runner?

ASH. What?

DOM. Like you did with him?

ASH. / No.

DOM. Is that why you're trying to save money? With this job?

ASH. No. I like having a job because I like having my own money.

,

DOM. It was better before.

ASH. Before when?

DOM. When you didn't have a job. We spent actual time together.

ASH. But this is a really good job. I'm handling original / documents

DOM. It's less than minimum wage. Your only colleague is a dyke from a cult. And also… well actually no. Nothing.

ASH. No, go on.

DOM. I'm finding it kind of… embarrassing that you're associating with all this… witch stuff.

After a stunned moment, ASH *laughs.*

ASH. Embarrassing?

DOM. Yeah it's a bit of an ick to be honest.

ASH. It's a bit of an ick? That loads of men murdered loads of women because they were scared of women ever being more powerful than men?

,

DOM. Well, whatever.

ASH. What Lily and I are doing is really important.

DOM. Okay sure. I just… where were you? This morning?

,

ASH. I went to see my mum.

DOM. Your mum?

ASH. Yeah.

DOM. Why?

ASH. Because. I never see her any more. Since moving here.

,

What?

DOM. Whenever you see her, you come back, and you're in a mood.

ASH. No I'm not. Not always.

,

She's stopped drinking.

DOM. Has she?

ASH. Yes.

,

DOM. Well I missed you. That's all.

,

And I had to feed Pan. You promised you would / do that.

ASH. I do feed Pan, this was just one time.

She pulls him into an embrace.

I'm not going to do a runner, okay?

I just like having my own money. So I can buy things.

DOM. What things?

ASH. Things for you.

DOM. Like what?

ASH (*shrugs*). Presents.

A nice watch?

DOM. You're gonna buy me a watch?

ASH (*kissing him*). Yeah, maybe. Maybe I'll buy you a car.

DOM (*kissing her back*). You're an idiot.

ASH. A big house? A space ship? Eternal life?

DOM. That sounds like a list of things Elon Musk wants.

They both laugh, the storm cloud has passed.

I don't need anything. I just want you.

ASH *is still laughing.*

I mean it. All the time. That's all I want.

ASH *stops laughing.*

He kisses her.

I love you.

ASH. I love you too.

He kisses her neck.

Then bites it. She flinches.

A flicker, like fire – something magic happens.

He draws blood.

Questions

A glitch in time.

An interrogation room.

A recording begins, stating the date and time.

ASH *and* LILY *drift between being the accuser and the accused.*

ASH. Do you drink?

LILY. A bit. A normal amount.

ASH. How many units per week, would you say?

LILY. Do you smoke?

ASH. Why is that relevant?

LILY. Do you ever smoke indoors?

ASH. No.

A normal amount?

LILY. Well I was drinking that night, to celebrate. Because I got the advance.

ASH. For your witch book?

LILY. Well, it's not a witch book. It's a political commentary on systemic injustice against women.

,

ASH. So you were celebrating… that. And you stayed until the club closed?

LILY. I would never normally stay out that late. She sort of, persuaded me.

ASH. So you didn't want to go?

LILY. No, I did, I did. I enjoyed it. In the end.

ASH. Do you go out together often?

LILY. Not out-out.

ASH. Drinks?

LILY. Drinks, yes. At the pub.

ASH. What did you drink at the pub?

LILY. I had a medium glass of house red. That's what I always have.

ASH. Are you close? You two?

LILY. Close?

They look at each other.

LILY. I think so. ASH. Not really.

,

ASH. Do you recognise this person?

LILY. Is that… / you?

ASH. This person?

LILY. What time was it, exactly? When you left the club?

ASH. It must have been half two, three-ish… I lost track of time.

LILY. You lost track of time? When you knew you had work the next day?

ASH. I always lose track of time. When I'm dancing.

LILY. Dancing. But not drinking?

ASH. It's my happy place.

LILY. Dancing?

ASH. Yeah.

LILY. Does alcohol have an effect on your memory?

ASH. I mean. Yeah. Of course it does… does it not have an effect on yours?

LILY. Do you smoke?

ASH. I can't see how that's relevant.

LILY. Do you ever smoke inside?

ASH. No.

LILY. Any naked flames inside?

Any prior convictions?

ASH. There was one thing...

LILY. What were you wearing? At The Level.

ASH. Are you serious?

LILY. I was naked.

ASH. I was naked.

LILY. Okay. Please don't waste our time.

ASH. No problem. Please don't waste mine.

ASH *turns to go, middle finger aloft.*

LILY. Had you seen the devil before that night?

ASH. Pardon?

LILY. Had you been to The Level before that night?

ASH. –

LILY. When did you last see him?

ASH. What?

LILY. / When?

ASH. When did you last see her?

LILY. She came in to work on Tuesday.

ASH. The day of the incident?

LILY. Yes.

ASH. Did you notice any unusual behaviour that day?

LILY. Not really. She was clearly distracted. But she's often distracted.

ASH. And you've had no contact since Tuesday?

LILY. None.

ASH. Is it alright if we take a little look at your phone. Just recent messages, emails.

LILY. There's really no need to do that.

ASH. It's just protocol, there's nothing to worry about.

LILY. I'm sorry, but that feels incredibly invasive.

ASH. So you're not willing to provide your phone?

LILY. I didn't realise I was the… I'm the one who reported her missing.

ASH. Look. We get a lot of these cases.

LILY. What cases?

ASH. It will be easier for you if you just cooperate.

Shower

LILY *is at the archive, glasses on, slippers on, listening to the radio. She is writing reference codes on box files* (*collection/group/series number*).

News on the radio: '…they were deployed in the early hours of June the eighth last year, to guard the crime scene in north-west London's Fryer Country Park where the bodies of the women were lying in situ, until the morning. Instead they chose – against all the rules – to breach the cordon, invade the crime scene and…'

The radio cuts out. Static.

The signal returns, but bad quality: 'it has come to the (*attention of the*) *investigative* (*response unit*) *that Miss Jackson, whose body was* (*discovered in her flat in Leyton*) *last Tuesday, suffered* (*with epilepsy*). *Coroners are working to* (*discover whether a*) *seizure could have led to* (*her drowning*)*.'*

ASH *arrives, unnoticed.*

LILY *jiggles the radio aerial but then it cuts out completely.*

ASH. Hi.

LILY (*still jiggling the aerial*). Oh hello. The radio just died.

There was a headline about the case.

Saying Taylor might have had a seizure, she suffered with /

ASH. I have those. Sometimes.

LILY. Do you?

ASH. Yeah. Epilepsy. I can dislocate from time.

LILY. Really?

ASH. Yeah.

LILY. Okay.

Well, let me know if there's anything I need to do, if that happens.

ASH. Oh. Not really.

LILY. Okay.

,

How was your weekend?

DOM *locking the door, recorded voices: 'What are you doing?' 'Locking the door.'*

ASH. Fine. I read the first half of a book, and then the first half of another book.

LILY. Well that's basically a whole book.

ASH. Yeah. I guess so.

ASH *logs into her computer.*

LILY. I had a really great night. The other night, at the… at the…

ASH. The Level.

LILY. Yeah. Just wanted to say thanks for… taking me out. Out-out.

ASH. Knew you'd like it.

LILY. Dancing like that. Just feels…

ASH. Free?

LILY. Yeah.

And um… about the other thing.

ASH. Oh don't worry about that.

LILY. Right.

ASH. We don't need to, you know, go into it.

LILY. Okay.

Understood.

LILY *hides her disappointment by logging into her computer.*

So I've spoken to Carmella's sister.

ASH. Oh! She agreed to speak to you?

LILY. Pardon.

ASH. No I just mean because she's so. Heartbroken. And angry.

LILY. Well I think it's *because* she's so angry that she wanted to speak to me.

ASH. Right. Yes.

,

LILY. So anyway, Daniella, the sister. Said Carmella had met this guy online. And she was, you know, (*Sotto.*) sending him pictures.

ASH. Well there's nothing wrong with that.

LILY. No I know. But she was staying up all night, making mistakes at work because she was so sleep deprived.

ASH. Well, you've probably never done it… but there's angles, make-up, lighting, underwear, background. It takes a long time. And skill.

LILY. I know what sexting is.

ASH. Have you done it?

LILY. Yes.

ASH. In the cult?

LILY. No, not in the cult. But more recently.

ASH. You've done recent sexting?

,

With who?

LILY. Nosy.

Refocussing on the case.

I spoke to a friend of Sara's too.

He said Sara was staying late in this pub every night. And so I spoke to the pub manager. And she said it was like Sara was waiting for someone. But she never met anyone, just waited there till the pub closed and then left.

ASH. So she wasn't waiting for anyone?

LILY. Maybe she was. But they never showed up. But just kept saying they would show up.

ASH. So she was being stood up?

LILY. She was being sleep deprived. She also started making mistakes at work. Turning up late. And then she actually got fired. And that day, the day she got fired, she went missing on her way home from work.

ASH. So they were all… tired. That's the link?

LILY. When people are tired –

ASH. We're all tired.

LILY. – they're easier to control. It's a form of torture.

ASH. Yeah, no I. I get that.

,

LILY. Do you want to see the photos?

ASH. What photos?

LILY (*getting the folder*). I've got the photos. Of the women.

ASH. How did you get these?

LILY. They all have these… they all have the same (mark) on / their necks

ASH. No. I don't. I don't want to see the photos.

LILY. No that's okay.

ASH. I just don't feel like looking at pictures of dead women today.

LILY. Sorry. Yes.

It's a lot.

She puts the folder down on the desk. They both look at the folder for a while.

I was thinking we should go there later.

ASH. Where?

LILY. To that pub. Where Sara went.

ASH. Shouldn't we leave the police to do that?

LILY. I'm not going to investigate. Just get a feel for the atmosphere.

Do you want to come?

ASH. No thanks. I'm knackered.

LILY. How come?

ASH. Coz Dom's on nights so I sort of… stay up.

LILY. So when do you sleep?

ASH. Well no, it's good because it means we get more quality time together.

,

,

LILY. Just come for one drink then.

ASH. Dom was in a bit of a mood. When we went out the other night.

LILY. Oh. Right.

ASH. So… yeah.

,

LILY. Hey, I nearly forgot… I um, got you a present.

ASH. Did you??

LILY. Just a little thing.

She hands ASH *the present. It is knitted slippers with a pom-pom on the toe to match Lily's own slippers.*

ASH *gasps.*

They're handmade. Same place / I got mine.

ASH. I love them!

She slips them on.

They're perfect.

They are perfect.

There is a possibility of a hug that doesn't happen.

LILY. I looked at your trainers so they're the same size…

LILY *takes off her slippers and puts her outdoor shoes on.*

Okay, I'm teaching now.

ASH. I'll join you next time, at the pub.

LILY. Okay.

ASH. I love these, Lily. Thank you.

LILY *smiles, heads out.*

ASH *admires her new slippers; something magic happens.*

But then a knock at the door.

DOM. Surprise!

He has flowers and a smart black duffle bag.

ASH. What you doing here?

DOM. Thought I'd meet you for lunch.

ASH. Why?

DOM. To say sorry. For flying off the handle.

ASH *takes the flowers.*

ASH. Thanks.

DOM (*looking around, opening drawers, taking up space*). You're right. It is pretty cool in here. What's that?

ASH. Those are thumb screws. Could you take your shoes off please?

DOM. Where's Lily?

ASH. She's teaching. Don't / touch those

DOM (*noticing Ash's slippers, laughs*). The fuck are those?

ASH. My slippers.

DOM *notices Lily's slippers.*

DOM. Whose are *they*?

ASH. Lily's.

DOM. Why have you got matching elf shoes?

ASH. They're indoor slippers.

We don't wear outdoor shoes in here.

They both look down at his shoes. He does not take them off.

DOM. Did you buy them?

ASH. Yeah.

DOM. If you needed indoor slippers I would have bought them for you.

DOM *picks up an apple which is on* ASH*'s desk.*

Why do they have a pom-pom?

He is about to take a bite of the apple.

ASH. Don't eat that.

DOM. Why? Does it contain the root of all evil?

ASH (*smiling*). No.

DOM. The source of all knowledge?

ASH (*laughing*). No. You just can't eat in here.

DOM (*laughing*). You don't like having me here, do you?

It's your special place –

ASH. No, it's just /

DOM. – for you and Lily.

,

(*Smiling.*) Always knew you were in the closet.

ASH (*laughing*). Stop it… let's just get lunch.

ASH *starts to take off her slippers.*

DOM. No.

ASH. What?

DOM. If we've got the place to ourselves…

…let's make the most of it.

He takes off his shoes.

ASH. What are you doing?

DOM (*geek voice*). I'm adhering to the rules of the archive.

He unbuttons his shirt.

ASH (*almost laughing*). Dom! Stop!

He kisses her.

DOM. Why?

ASH. Because. We've got a flat we can have sex in anytime.

DOM. But this is more fun.

ASH. Lily will be back soon.

DOM. Fuck Lily. Who gives a fuck about Lily?

ASH. I do.

He starts undressing her.

DOM. Well who do you give more of a fuck about?

ASH. Well, you obviously.

DOM. And who's the one that's just brought you flowers.

ASH (*wriggling away*). Well, I don't need flowers, I need to work.

He is affronted, upset.

DOM (*buttoning his shirt back up, sotto*). Fine. / Sorry.

ASH. No. Sorry, I didn't mean that. They're lovely. The flowers.

DOM. I'm trying to be spontaneous. You're always saying 'be more fun' and I'm trying.

ASH. Okay okay. It is fun. I just need to like, shift gears. From work brain into…

Come here.

She is sitting on the desk. He goes over to her, in between her legs. They kiss.

Yeah, no this is fun, actually.

They kiss more.

The radio comes on, a distorted male voice (DOM*'s*) *listing names: 'Heather Cooper, Janet Methven, Natalie Esack.'*

ASH *pulls away.*

DOM. What? What's wrong?

ASH. Did you say something?

DOM. No.

ASH *looks over to the radio, freaked out.*

She turns the radio off.

Are there showers here?

ASH. Yeah. Through there.

DOM. Come on.

He leads her to the bathroom.

Behind frosted glass, he turns on the shower. Steam rises.

Their silhouettes, together, kissing, pulsating.

Heavy breathing, choking and spluttering.

Slowly, the water turns red like blood.

ASH *is drowning in the water.*

ASH. Can't breathe.

DOM. What?

ASH. I can't breathe.

DOM. I can't hear you.

ASH. I can't breathe.

DOM. Don't come in tomorrow.

ASH *gasps for breath.*

Stay at home, with me.

ASH. Okay.

DOM. Promise.

ASH. Yes.

He stops.

He turns the shower off.

They come out from behind the glass.

ASH *is drenched, make-up streaming.* DOM *is, somehow, dry.*

He laughs.

DOM. You look mental.

He gets out his phone. Puts an arm round her shoulders.

He takes a selfie of the two of them.

He looks at the photo.

See, that was fun, right?

Ash?

ASH. Yeah it was fun.

DOM *checks his watch.*

DOM. I'm on shift now.

Can you sort dinner tonight?

ASH. Yeah.

He goes to his bag. Piece by piece, he puts on his pristine and perfectly pressed uniform.

When he is dressed, we see that he is a police officer.

He glows.

He notices the folder on Lily's desk.

DOM. What's that?

ASH. Nothing. It's Lily's.

DOM *picks up the folder, opens it.*

He looks at the photographs of the murdered women for an uncomfortably long time.

DOM. How did she get this?

ASH *shrugs.*

She shouldn't have this.

He puts the folder in his bag.

He kisses ASH.

He leaves.

ASH *stands motionless, in shock and confusion, then leaves in the opposite direction.*

ACT TWO

Thumb

Next day, LILY *at the archive, making notes from an ancient-looking book, wearing her work slippers, listening to the radio.*

News on the radio: 'Were you given a description? Of the pictures? No, we refused. We've never never seen the images. I was broken anyway, but at that point, I started having – and I still have them – images of what I think they look like, in the pictures.'

LILY *stops. She reaches for the folder with the photos in. But it's not there.*

She looks around for it. Can't find it. Calls Ash. It rings for a long time.

And finally, click: DOM, *still in his uniform, answers the call. He is holding Pan.*

LILY. Ash? DOM. Hello?

LILY. Oh. Sorry. Hi. Think I've got the wrong number.

DOM. Who is this?

LILY. It's Lily. From the archive. Is that… Dom?

DOM (*turning on the charm*). Yeah. Hi Lily. I'm so sorry we haven't got those clothes back to you.

LILY. Oh honestly, no rush. I was just trying to get hold of Ash.

DOM. Right.

LILY. Yeah she was actually meant to be here about an hour ago. So I'm not quite sure…

DOM. Oh she's not coming in today.

LILY. Oh really? But she messaged me.

DOM. Did she? When?

,

LILY. Could I just speak to her quickly? It's quite important.

DOM. She's asleep.

LILY. It's midday.

DOM. Yeah. She's sick.

Anything I can pass on to her?

LILY. It's just about some documents. That were on my desk.

DOM. What documents?

LILY *is perplexed.*

LILY. Could you just ask her to call me once she's woken up?

,

DOM. Sure. Thanks, Lily.

He hangs up.

LILY (*sotto*). So weird.

She locks the phone. Exits.

ASH *appears in the flat* (*dry now*). *She takes her phone off* DOM.

ASH. Did you answer my phone?

DOM. Why is she calling you at home?

ASH. Who?

DOM. Have you messaged her?

ASH. Lily?

DOM. Yes, Lily.

ASH. A bit. I mean. Just work stuff.

DOM. What work stuff?

ASH. She's my boss.

DOM. How often do you text her?

ASH. A normal amount?

DOM. Can you unlock your phone?

,

ASH. Are you serious?

DOM. Unlock it.

ASH. No. That's… no.

He steps towards her.

Dom, seriously.

Pan bites him.

DOM. Ow. Fuck.

He fucking bit me.

ASH *takes Pan.*

Give me your thumb.

ASH. What?

DOM. Your thumbprint. To unlock it.

He grabs her hand. She pulls away.

ASH. No. Fuck off.

DOM. Give me your thumb or I'll break it.

,

Slowly, she presses her thumb to the phone.

The phone unlocks.

He reads through her messages for a long time, scrolling, scrolling. ASH *watches in silence. When he has read them all, he throws the phone down,* ASH *picks it up, puts it in her pocket.* DOM *starts putting things in a bag, like nothing happened.*

Do you want to go to the pond?

ASH. What?

DOM. Have a swim.

ASH. Now?

DOM. Yeah.

,

ASH. Aren't you meant to be at work?

DOM. No, it's my day off.

Thank god. Fucking carnage there.

ASH. At the station?

DOM. There's some footage missing.

ASH. Oh.

,

What's the footage of?

DOM. Can't say.

ASH. So someone's hiding it?

DOM (*packing the swimming bag*). Can't say.

ASH. Someone in your team?

DOM. Babe. I can't say.

ASH. What does the Inspector reckon?

DOM. Well he's off, isn't he.

ASH. Is he?

DOM. Compassionate leave.

ASH. Oh right.

DOM. Yeah I told you. His girlfriend died.

ASH. Fuck. What?

Roderick's girlfriend died?

DOM. Yeah. I told you.

He didn't tell her.

,

Anyway. I've got snacks, suncream, your bikini, my bikini, towels.

To the pond!

ASH *is not quite convinced.*

What?

ASH. I don't want to go.

DOM. Why?

ASH. Because… because last time we went there you got stung by that / bee and it was

DOM. I've packed *two* EpiPens. Two.

ASH. Okay.

Well good. Fine.

DOM. To the pond!

He puts the now-ready backpack on.

Binoculars

LILY *goes to the police station.* ASH *is the* OFFICER.

LILY. Hi.

OFFICER. How can I help?

LILY. I'm Lily. I'm the external research expert on the investigation. Into the deaths of Ms Riccardo, Ms Ustinov and Miss Jackson.

Lily Holmes?

OFFICER (*writing down*). Lily. Holmes.

LILY. I sent through my report as a password protected PDF, but I also have this hard copy, if that's useful.

OFFICER. Give me the headline, for now.

LILY. Well I've been studying ritualistic murders for, well for most of my career. And there are signs of ritual across the cases. All three women had marks on their necks which are not associated with asphyxiation. Also all three women, as you already know, were working class and had prior convictions, of varying degrees. And there are indications of ritualistic punishment, for example Taylor Jackson's thumbs were broken. But she had no other injuries at all.

OFFICER. We're not dealing with the case of Miss Jackson, I'm afraid.

LILY. Why not?

OFFICER. Because the incident occurred in Leyton. We're Southwark.

LILY. But the three cases could be linked. That's the whole point.

OFFICER. No, I know, but to discuss Miss Jackson's case, you need to head to Waltham Forest Police Station. Which is…

The OFFICER *writes down the address.*

… here.

LILY *takes the piece of paper.*

LILY. On the forensic report there was also evidence of sexual assault. Across the cases. So it's possible a DNA match could be / found if we act quickly

OFFICER. We haven't been able to collate any significant evidence in regards to sexual assault. And again, with the case of Miss Jackson, that'll be Waltham Forest.

,

We also can't accept that hard copy of the report.

LILY. Oh.

OFFICER. We're paperless.

LILY. Okay.

,

Well. The bottom line is. I believe that the cases are linked.

This does not have the dramatic effect that LILY *intended.*

Okay?

OFFICER. Okay. We'll bear that in mind.

Is there anything else I can help you with?

LILY. No. That's my… those are my findings.

OFFICER. Well thank you for your work and we'll be in touch shortly.

,

LILY. There is something else actually.

,

I've got this friend.

OFFICER. Well I've heard that one before.

LILY. No really, I've got this friend. And was just wondering. How long does somebody need to be missing to be considered a missing person?

OFFICER. How long has your friend been missing?

LILY. A week.

,

OFFICER. Do you want to come through and take a seat?

In the reporting room, they sit. The OFFICER *waits patiently for* LILY *to start.*

LILY. She's missed four days of work.

OFFICER. So she's a work colleague?

LILY. Yeah. She's actually working on the investigation with me.

She's signed the DNA. The NDA.

,

I've been messaging her but…

OFFICER. She's at the pond.

LILY. Pardon?

OFFICER. She doesn't respond?

LILY. What?

OFFICER. To your messages. She doesn't respond?

LILY. No. Not for a while now. I think she might be trapped inside her flat.

,

OFFICER. So you do know where she is…

LILY. Well I drove past her flat, and I saw her.

OFFICER. You drove past her flat?

LILY. Yeah.

OFFICER. Intentionally? Or were you just passing through?

LILY. No it was, yeah, a slight detour.

OFFICER. And you waited outside the flat until you had a clear sighting?

LILY. Yes.

OFFICER. A block of flats or a maisonette?

LILY. A block.

OFFICER. What floor is she on?

LILY. Third floor.

OFFICER. So how did you get a clear sighting of her from street level?

LILY. I had binoculars.

,

OFFICER. Did you bring binoculars especially?

LILY. No I I I always have binoculars in my car. For bird watching.

OFFICER. Because Southwark is famous for it's bird watching.

LILY. There are actually. In Burgess Park. Some quite rare warblers. Sedge warblers nesting under the… (*She trails off.*)

,

OFFICER. So you took a detour to her place, waited outside – on the street or in your car?

LILY. In my car.

OFFICER. In your car, and looked at her through the binoculars that you use for bird watching.

LILY. Yes.

OFFICER. And what was she doing, when you saw her?

LILY. The first time, she was dancing.

OFFICER. The first time? How many times have you done this?

LILY. A couple of times.

,

Three times.

OFFICER. Three times.

Just explain to me again what your relationship is with this woman?

LILY. We work together.

OFFICER. Have you been to each other's homes before?

LILY. No.

OFFICER. So how did you get her address?

LILY. Look – you're focussing on the wrong details here. She was dancing… but in a trance or something. Her eyes were rolled back.

OFFICER. Right. And the next time? What was she doing?

LILY. The next time… it sort of looked like… looked like she had tape over her mouth.

OFFICER. Tape?

LILY. I think so. Or something like that.

It could have been a gag. Or a scarf.

My scarf actually.

OFFICER. Well to be honest, Libby.

LILY. Lily.

OFFICER. Lily. None of this is enough cause for concern.

LILY. But she's missing.

OFFICER. Well she's not missing, if she's in her flat.

LILY. It just looked… I've just / got this feeling

OFFICER. We can't report someone missing, if they're just dancing in their flat, wearing a scarf.

LILY. No. Look. I've got a strong feeling that something is wrong.

OFFICER. What's her name?

LILY. Aisling Toft.

The OFFICER *recognises the name.*

A beat – before she types it in.

OFFICER. We have her on record.

LILY. Oh. So things have happened before?

OFFICER. No. She has a criminal record.

LILY. Oh. What for?

OFFICER. I can't disclose that.

,

If any further cause for concern comes up, do come back in. With her.

LILY. Okay. Thank you.

,

OFFICER. Do you want to go for a drink?

LILY. Pardon?

OFFICER. Do you want to have a think?

LILY. I will do, yes.

LILY *gets up.*

OFFICER. And Libby?

LILY *stops.*

It's not best practice to go to your colleagues' homes without their permission.

LILY. That's not what /

OFFICER. I'd recommend that you refrain from doing that.

LILY *turns to leave again.*

(*Sotto.*) She's lying.

LILY. Pardon?

OFFICER. She's fine. Your friend.

I'm sure she's fine.

Holiday

LILY *in the pub, medium house red. She's watching the news on her phone.*

The news: 'The evidence seen by the inquiry meant that failures in recruitment and vetting meant he was able to continue a policing career which should have been denied to him.'

While LILY *is watching the news,* ASH *gets Pan and whispers to him.*

The news continues but underwatery.

ASH *enters the pub.*

ASH. Sorry.

Am I late?

LILY. Where are your shoes?

ASH. What shoes?

,

LILY. Do you want a drink?

A lime and soda?

LILY *goes off to the bar.*

ASH *gets a tea towel from her bag and dries her hands and feet.*

Then she gets Pantalaimon out and puts him on the table.

She feeds him some dandelion flowers.

LILY *returns with the drinks, but seeing Pan causes her to recoil.*

What?! No. Not?

ASH (*not looking up from feeding Pan*). This is my rabbit.

LILY (*regarding Pan as a creature from the depths of the underworld*). What?

Why is it in the pub?

ASH. Because. I had to bring him with me.

LILY. Why is it on the table?

ASH. Because I need to feed him.

LILY. Does he bite?

,

ASH. He won't bite you.

LILY *sits down, leaning her body as far away from the rabbit as possible.*

You're quite weird you know.

LILY. (!)

ASH. Leaving me a note like that.

LILY. You're… (feeding a rabbit, in a pub.)

ASH. Leaving me a note like a Jane Austen character.

LILY. Well you weren't answering my messages.

,

(*Sotto.*) Did you have to break out of the flat?

ASH. What?

LILY (*sotto*). To come here. And meet me.

ASH. No.

,

Do you want to stroke him? He's very soft.

LILY. No thank you.

,

Why aren't you wearing shoes?

ASH. Went swimming.

LILY. What?

ASH. At the pond. With Dom.

LILY. At the pond?

ASH. Guess what he did?

LILY. What? What did he do? Are you okay?

ASH. What?

LILY. You look different.

ASH. Different good or different bad?

LILY. Did something happen at the pond?

ASH. Yes, I'm trying to tell you.

LILY. Sorry. Yes.

ASH. He swam up to me and said, 'I've got a surprise.'

LILY. Oh god.

ASH. In the water. Treading water.

And then he said, 'Morocco. Beach Resort. Ten days.'

LILY. What?

ASH (*the hugest smile*). For our anniversary. Can you believe it?

LILY. / No.

ASH. That I have a man in my life who does things like this.

And we were far out, totally alone, in the deepest bit of the pond and I was so excited, I was laughing so much I was like drowning and it was so cold, our breath coming out like dragons.

It was really special.

LILY*'s face is deep in thought.*

LILY. How come he answered your phone?

The comment hangs strangely in the air. ASH *ignores it.*

ASH. And Pan was there too. Our baby.

LILY. The rabbit?

ASH. In the pond.

LILY. You're lying.

ASH. What?!

LILY. Rabbits can't swim.

ASH. Rabbits love swimming.

And so do I. And so does Dom actually. And we'll be doing lots of swimming in Morocco because our hotel is right on the beach. Why are you being so weird?

LILY. What about work?

ASH. He's booked it off. And he's made arrangements with Skye's mum, she's got her sister coming / to help

LILY. I mean your work, our work.

ASH. Well yeah, that's why I came to meet you –

LILY. Right.

ASH. – to ask you what the deal is with my annual leave?

LILY. You don't have any annual leave. You're a temp.

,

ASH. I thought I was the deputy expert.

LILY. Well now you're just someone who wants to drop it all to go to Morocco.

,

What happened to the photo folder?

ASH. What?

LILY. The folder. With the photos of the women's bodies.

ASH. I don't know.

LILY. Did you take it?

ASH. No.

,

LILY. Do you have a criminal record?

,

ASH. Are you jealous? That I'm going away with Dom?

,

LILY. You can't just miss a week of work and then ask for ten more days off.

,

ASH. Okay. I just thought you'd be a bit more chill. About this.

LILY. Well I'm not chill, okay, I'm not chill.

,

ASH. Do you have something against Dom? Because if you do, you should just say.

LILY. I just don't think it's a good idea. This holiday.

It's not going to work, I'm afraid.

,

ASH. I think Dom was right.

DOM *places a candle on their table.*

LILY. About what?

ASH. About you.

ASH *leaves, with Pan.*

Desire

Back at the flat, ASH *is surrounded by candles.*

She puts Pan into his hutch.

DOM *appears.*

They stand there, looking at each other amongst the candles.

After a moment of stillness, she goes to him.

He holds her face. Kisses all down her neck. Envelops her in his arms.

Together, they sink to the floor, where they become animals, on their hands and knees, sniffing each other, circling each other.

Their faces connect, they kiss.

DOM *climbs on top of* ASH *and they breathe together for a moment, but then –*

The lights strobe, making it hard to decipher what is happening.

Animalistic movement.

Then ASH *is gone.*

For a moment, it's just DOM.

Blackout.

Fire

ASH *is at the archive, studying a document, slippers on.*

The only light is a lit candle on her desk.

She hears LILY *coming in.*

She blows out the candle and turns on the main light.

LILY *comes in, takes off her shoes. Puts on her slippers.*

She is surprised to see ASH.

LILY. Oh! Hi.

Didn't know if you'd be here…

ASH. Well I am here. If that's okay.

LILY (*as if she doesn't care*). Sure.

ASH*'s phone rings. She silences it.*

LILY *settles into her desk and they both work in silence for a bit.*

ASH. Can I ask you something?

LILY *looks up from her work.*

Did the police really ask you to work on the case?

,

LILY. What do you mean?

ASH. I just don't really understand why they would need your involvement.

LILY. Well, Ash, if you don't think we're doing valuable work here, you don't have to be here.

ASH*'s phone rings, she silences it.*

,

(*Referring to the document* ASH *is looking at.*) What's that?

ASH. The cause of Taylor's death was asphyxia – drowning.

LILY. I know.

ASH. But she was found in her flat.

The only way you could drown in your own flat is in the bath. But she didn't have a bathtub. Only a shower, see?

As ASH *points to the document,* LILY *notices bruises around her wrists.*

LILY. What is that?

ASH. It's the floor plan of her flat. So that means she drowned elsewhere / and then her body was

LILY. No what is that. On your wrists?

ASH *covers them up. The silence lasts a long time.*

We need to talk.

ASH. About Kevin?

LILY. What?

ASH. Nothing. Sorry. The book.

LILY. I just want to talk. About some stuff.

ASH. Are you going to fire me?

LILY. No.

ASH. Are you going to ask me out?

LILY. No. What? I'm, no.

I just – need to say. Something.

I, um, when you were off work I got a bit concerned and I went round to your flat. And I feel like I have to bring it up I I feel like I'm the only person who's noticed, the only person who sees you regularly. I really don't want to make you feel awkward. I just, haven't known how to… But now… with these bruises on your wrists and…

ASH. You came to my flat?

LILY. I know it was weird –

ASH. Did you go there intentionally? Or were you just passing through?

LILY. I've been keeping notes. Of times when I've observed that you might be at risk.

ASH. What notes?

LILY. Because that's what you're meant to do.

She produces the notes. ASH *reads them.*

When you're concerned about a friend or colleague. Because often in traumatic situations, they don't remember.

ASH (*referring to the notes*). This is really invasive.

LILY. I know it seems that way but I'm not trying to –

ASH. Why have you done this?

LILY. I'm just trying to document things.

,

ASH. Are you trying to get me to break up with Dom?

LILY (*blurting it out*). You had that thing. That mark on your (neck).

A stunned silence.

ASH *gets up, kicks off her slippers. Begins to put her trainers on.*

ASH. No. Fuck. You're being so fucking weird.

LILY. I think you might be in danger.

ASH. You're not a fucking fortune teller, Lily.

,

LILY (*attempting calm*). I think it would be a good idea to take pictures of those bruises.

ASH *is now putting her jacket on.*

It's recommended, to have evidence, of… ongoing… patterns. Of behaviour.

So that, if you ever need to get the police involved /

ASH *laughs.*

I hope this is okay for me to say, but –

ASH. It's not.

LILY. What?

ASH. It's not okay for you to say.

So could you just. Not say.

LILY. But he's hurting you.

ASH. That's just from the sex we have.

LILY. –

ASH. I'm fine!

I'm fucking fine, okay? And happy.

LILY. Okay.

ASH. Not everyone is a victim.

LILY. That's not what I'm saying.

ASH. What are you saying then?

What are you saying?!

LILY. –

ASH. If you don't have anything nice to say…

Then just shut the fuck up.

Is how the saying goes, I believe.

ASH *puts her trainers on, facing away from* LILY.

LILY. I'm not good at this. Conversations like this.

I'm teaching now, so. Could you just. Stay here. And we can talk later.

ASH. Stay here?

LILY. And we can talk later. Please stay.

LILY *leaves.*

ASH *reads the rest of the notes. She hates them, she's angry and crying.*

ASH. Pan?

Pan's hutch lights up, as if summoned.

ASH *goes to the hutch and gets Pan out. She holds onto him and breathes, calming down.*

You are lovely and I love you.

She puts him back in the hutch, and gets her candle and a box of matches out of her desk drawer.

She strikes a match, lights the candle. Pan's hutch glows red.

The whispers again, but louder and clearer this time: 'Victoria Rose, 2013; Emma Siswick, 2014; Jill Goldsmith, 2015.'

ASH *holds the notes over the candle flame, but then she changes her mind, retracts them.*

She looks at her wrists. Strokes the bruises. She starts taking off her clothes.

She hesitates for a moment, then picks up her phone and takes photos of bruises on her wrists and stomach.

Meanwhile, unnoticed by ASH, *the archive fills with smoke. The notes have set fire. Other things have set fire, flames spring up at random.*

The whispers compete with the sound of the fire: 'Alice Farquharson, 2019; Claire Parry, 2020; Sarah Everard, Bibaa Henry, Nicole Smallman, 2021.'

More flames spread. Smoke thickens.

Pan?

Help!

Fire!

The lights flicker and sputter, and then blackout.

ACT THREE

Police

Outside the archive. Smoke and ash.

Through the haze, blue and red lights. Sirens, getting closer.

LILY, *in a state of panic.*

The police arrive at the scene.

DOM, *in police uniform.*

LILY. Dom?

(*Referring to his uniform.*) What's this?

DOM. What?

LILY. What are you wearing?

DOM *looks down at his clothes, deeply confused.*

Are you a police officer?

DOM. No, I'm a stripper.

LILY. Ash never said...

DOM. Lily this is serious. Where's Ash?

LILY. I told her to stay inside.

Oh fuck… is she inside? Oh my god. Oh god! Ash.

DOM. Lily, you cannot enter the premises.

LILY. But is she inside? Is she?

DOM. Here. Let's just step away from the site. They'll be cordoning off this whole area.

He gently guides her away from the site.

The fire marshals have checked. No one's inside, no one's at risk. We need to wait for the all clear, from the smoke and carbon particles. The investigative team will inspect the building in a few days. Entrances, exits...

LILY. Why are you here?

DOM. I need to ask a few questions.

LILY. Where's… where's the rest of your unit?

DOM. I just said. They're round the back, securing the area.

,

LILY. Is Ash safe?

DOM. We don't currently know.

LILY. What?!

DOM. Her whereabouts is currently unknown.

LILY. Oh god.

Why are you so calm?

DOM (*sotto, close to her*). Because I'm at work, and I need to focus.

Okay?

LILY *nods.*

But as someone who loves Ash, of course I'm worried. Of course I am.

LILY. We need to look for her.

DOM. I've got a team out looking for her. All of my best people. They'll find her.

LILY. But they don't know her.

DOM. (And you do?)

,

She'll turn up.

She always does.

LILY. What do you mean, she always does?

,

DOM. We need to establish a few details.

,

Lily?

It's okay, I just need to establish a timeline.

Has there been any recent electrical faults or repairs in the building?

LILY. Not that I… actually we've had some issues with the radio.

DOM. The radio?

LILY. Yeah. The signal's been coming in and out so… maybe the power socket… I should have got that fixed. Stupid stupid idiot.

Doubtfully, DOM *notes this down, and moves on.*

DOM. Who has access to this section of the archive?

LILY. Just me. And Ash.

DOM. Any recent disputes?

LILY. With Ash?

DOM. With anyone.

LILY. No, not really.

DOM. Not really or no?

,

I'm just trying to rule out the possibility of arson.

LILY. Arson? It wasn't arson.

,

Ash was the only person here.

DOM *laughs.*

DOM. You think you know her?

LILY. Pardon?

DOM. You don't know her. She's…

He laughs again.

LILY. What? What is she?

DOM. She's just Ash. This is what she does.

More Questions

A glitch in time.

An interrogation room.

A recording begins, stating the date and time.

ASH, LILY *and* DOM *drift between being the accuser and the accused.*

ASH (*showing a mugshot*). Do you recognise this person?

LILY. Is that… / you?

DOM. This person?

LILY. No.

ASH. I always lose track of time. When I'm dancing.

It's my happy place.

DOM. Dancing?

ASH. Yeah.

DOM. Drinking?

ASH. No.

DOM. Do you smoke?

LILY. No.

DOM. She went in to work on Tuesday.

LILY *and* DOM. Yes.

ASH. Did you notice any unusual behaviour that day?

,

LILY *and* DOM. We had an argument.

ASH. An argument?

,

DOM. Are you close? You two?

LILY. Close?

They look at each other.

LILY. Not really. ASH. I think so.

,

DOM. Look. We get a lot of these cases.

ASH. What cases?

LILY. You should be careful.

ASH. Why?

LILY. Just. Be careful.

Doorstep

ASH *is on* LILY*'s doorstep.*

She rings the doorbell.

After a while, LILY *comes to the door.*

ASH *has a manic, urgent energy.*

ASH. Hi.

LILY. Where've you been?

ASH. It wasn't me Lily, I promise. Something happened in the archive. There was no fire. And then, there was a fire. Out of nowhere.

I took the photos. Like you said.

LILY. All my work is gone.

I was trying to keep those women alive. Those women who were executed in a regressive justice system. Because it's still happening. It's still regressive.

ASH. I was scared Dom might read the notes.

LILY. Oh poor Dom god forbid that he should read the notes.

ASH. (I'm sorry.)

LILY. He should read them. He should fucking read them –

Why didn't you tell me he was a police officer?

ASH. It just never came up.

LILY. I was working directly with the police.

ASH. (Were you?)

LILY. I feel like I don't know you at all.

Do you even have a PhD?

I've never been able to find any evidence of it.

ASH. Well if you come round to my flat again with your binoculars, you can see the certificate on the wall.

An impasse.

,

,

LILY. Bad things happen around you.

ASH. What?

LILY. You suck all the bad things towards you.

ASH. I… I don't…

LILY. I should never have let you in. I usually don't let people in.

,

ASH. Are you firing me?

LILY. I think if you burn down your workplace you're, automatically fired.

ASH. Lily, please. I'm really scared.

LILY. I've got nothing now.

ASH. I'm sorry!

LILY. It was very stupid of me to think I could help you.

ASH. You can help me. Please.

,

LILY. The investigation has concluded. No ritualistic murders. No links. Taylor did have a seizure – in the shower and that's how she's drowned. The cause of the fire at Carmella's flat was an electrical fault. Sara hanged herself.

,

,

ASH. But what about all those footprints? Around the tree?

LILY. Those were all her own footprints –

ASH. But what about the marks, on their necks?

LILY. Ash. The investigation has concluded.

It's over.

ASH. It's not over. What / about me?

LILY. You've taken the photos.

You can get out now.

It's over.

Alibi

ASH *sits on the sofa, holding Pan, singing a love song to him.*

The sound of a bee.

ASH *does not react to the bee, just continues sitting calmly with Pan.*

A key in the door.

DOM *comes in.* ASH *and* DOM *stare at each other.*

DOM. Where have you been?

She stands up, embraces him.

ASH. Were you looking for me?

DOM. Lots of people are looking for you.

ASH. Careful.

DOM. What?

ASH. Just be careful. There's a bee.

The bee swoops towards DOM.

He bats it away.

Careful!

He kills it against the wall with a book.

Dom!

DOM. What?! I'm allergic.

ASH. I know, I was going to get it in a glass, take it outside.

ASH *takes Pan and puts him safely into his hutch.*

DOM. Were you with Lily?

ASH. No.

DOM. Charlie?

ASH. No. Dom, he nearly killed me, for fuck's sake.

,

DOM. So where were you then?

ASH. I was trying to protect us. Lily made all these notes.

DOM. What notes?

ASH. Horrible things, that were totally twisted from the truth.

I was going to burn them.

DOM. Burn what?

ASH. The notes.

DOM. At the archive?

ASH. Yeah…

DOM. Inside the archive?

ASH. (Yeah.)

DOM. So it was you?

ASH. No. It wasn't. It it was like the fire was… like it had been there all along.

DOM *puts his head in his hands.*

DOM. You and Lily have an argument.

The place goes up in flames.

You disappear.

It doesn't look good.

,

It's ten years, Ash. Ten years for arson –

ASH. Well it wasn't, / wasn't arson.

DOM. – give or take, depending on the category of culpability and the category of harm.

ASH. What?

DOM. Culpability is whether the fire was lit on purpose with intention – / which it was.

ASH. / No it wasn't.

DOM. Harm is how much harm was caused either to life, or property – which there was.

ASH. Harm to life? Was anyone /

DOM. No – harm to property, Ash. The archive. Lots of that old shit is irreplaceable right?

,

ASH. It's all irreplaceable. It's an archive.

DOM. So probably category two for harm.

On top of all your other shit.

ASH *puts her head in her hands.*

ASH. She's completely heartbroken.

DOM. So you were with her.

ASH. No I no. She didn't let me in. She fired me.

This pleases DOM *slightly.*

DOM. Did she?

ASH *is crying. He pulls her into an embrace.*

Hey, hey, it's okay. I can fix this. Okay? We can fix this.

ASH. How?

DOM. The investigative team are still waiting for clearance from the fire marshals. So I've got a window. To get there first.

What did you use to start the fire?

ASH. I didn't start the fire.

DOM. What did you use?

ASH. My candle.

DOM. What candle?

ASH. My scented candle.

DOM. / Okay.

ASH. Nordic Pinewood.

DOM. Okay. So I'll remove your candle.

They will need to interview you, because you work there.

I'll prep you for the interview, we'll create an alibi.

We'll say you were home from work before the fire started.

ASH. But Lily knows I was there.

DOM. They're not going to ask questions, Ash. These people are my friends.

,

ASH. Doesn't this put you at risk? Of of… collusion or something?

DOM. Yeah. It does.

,

ASH. Have you done stuff like this before? Covering stuff up?

DOM. No.

Only for you.

,

ASH. This is your thing, isn't it?

Rescuing me.

He kisses her so softly, kisses her eyes, wipes her tears, kisses her cheek.

DOM. You know what I always do in situations like this?

I look for the silver lining.

ASH *scoffs.*

ASH. I can't see / how

DOM. Morocco.

If she's fired you. You don't even need annual leave.

ASH *smiles.*

See?

I'll fix this. I promise.

ASH. Okay. Thank you.

'

I'm going to try get some sleep.

ASH *exits.*

On the table, ASH*'s phone pings.* DOM *considers taking the phone to her, but then changes his mind and enters her passcode.*

A voice note from LILY. *He listens to it.*

LILY. Hey Ash it's me. I've recorded this about seven times and yeah I'm just finding it hard to… I'm still angry. That hasn't gone away. But I also bloody can't stop bloody thinking about you. Which is very illogical and and annoying. To have you, in my head, all the time.

I think when you came to my door I wasn't really listening to you. Because I was, I still am, grieving all my work and and… but you said you were scared. And that keeps going and going in my head and I can't stop…

So I just wanted to say – and I really don't want this to come across invasive like before – but if you send me the photos, I'd be happy to take them to the police for you. Because obviously, with Dom being there…

So yes. No pressure. Just send them through. If you want to.

You are still fired though. Just to be clear.

DOM *deletes the voice note.*

He puts the phone in a drawer and locks it. He puts the key on a chain around his neck.

Skye

LILY *and* DOM *wander separately through the charred and blackened archive.* DOM *finds the candle.*

ASH *has been in the flat for days. She takes Pan over to the window.*

ASH (*sotto, to Pan*). So here's the window and look those are the trees and that's the other block that's the same as this block. And that's the playground. And that puddle's still there. On the slide. It's been exactly the same puddle for days.

Oh and there's Dom coming home. So you go to bed.

She returns him to his hutch.

Nice and safe and cosy in bed because I love you.

Ash does her hair.

DOM *comes barrelling, bouncing, happy. He picks her up, swings her round, kisses her.*

ASH *squeals with the adrenaline love rush of it.*

Hello.

DOM. Just wanted to do that.

As you were.

ASH. You ruined my braid.

DOM. Why you doing your hair?

ASH. To look nice?

DOM. You do look nice.

You look beautiful actually.

She kisses him.

Guess what?

ASH. What?

DOM. I'm up for a promotion.

ASH *gasps.*

Inspector.

ASH. What about Roderick?

DOM. Roderick's leaving. The hearing didn't go in his favour.

ASH. What hearing?

DOM. I told you about the hearing.

ASH. I thought he was on compassionate leave?

DOM*'s voice goes weird.*

DOM. He was on a probationary period, and now…

(*Pointing to himself.*) Inspector Dominic De Luca.

ASH. I don't feel good.

DOM. Sounds good right?

ASH. –

Over the following, DOM *is blowing up a pair of* Frozen-*branded arm bands.*

DOM. It's a big pay rise. We could move into a bigger place.

ASH. I've been in here for too long.

DOM. Yeah we need more space. And I could start a university fund for Skye.

Give her a head start.

And I'll be able to brush the archive thing under the carpet. No questions.

ASH. I need fresh air.

DOM. Open the window if you want fresh air.

He continues blowing up the arm bands.

DOM*'s voice returns to normal.*

I'm taking Skye swimming.

She can swim across the whole pool now.

She's the best in the class.

,

ASH. Can I come with you?

DOM. What?

ASH. To the swimming lesson.

DOM *continues blowing the arm bands.*

DOM. Maybe another time. Not today.

ASH (*disappointed*). Okay.

,

DOM. What?

ASH. When are you going to let me meet her?

DOM. She's little. I don't want to confuse her.

DOM *continues blowing the arm bands.*

ASH. Why are you blowing them up now?

DOM. What?

ASH. Why don't you blow them up when you get there?

DOM. Because it saves time.

ASH. Does she even need them?

DOM. What?

ASH. If she can swim across the whole pool, does she need the arm bands?

DOM. What are you asking?

ASH. Show me a photo of her. A recent one.

,

DOM (*close to her face*). You're losing it, do you know that?

I'll be back at two-ish.

DOM *is getting ready to leave.*

ASH. Shall I get started with the packing?

DOM. What?

ASH. For Morocco.

DOM. Oh. Yeah okay.

ASH. Do you want to share the big suitcase or do two separate bags?

DOM. Dunno, check the baggage thing.

,

ASH. Can I have my phone then?

DOM *hesitates.*

DOM. Just use the two smaller bags. It's fine.

ASH. But I'll still need to check the measurements. All the airlines have different rules.

He doesn't want to give her the phone.

I won't message anyone.

He goes to the drawer. Unlocks it.

He hands her the phone.

DOM. I'll know. If you message someone.

ASH. I won't.

,

DOM *leaves.*

In the bedroom, with shaking hands, she takes a photo of a new bruise, on her neck.

Photos

LILY *goes into the police station.* ASH *is the* OFFICER.

LILY. Hi.

OFFICER. Ah. You again.

LILY. Yeah. Libby.

OFFICER. It's Lily, isn't it?

LILY. No it is, yeah. I was just –

OFFICER. If you report a crime under a pseudonym / it reduces the chance of

LILY. No I was just. It was a joke. Because last time you thought my name was Libby.

,

OFFICER. Thanks for your report.

Unfortunately the investigation has already concluded.

LILY. No, I know. It just… feels a bit. Doesn't feel right.

OFFICER. Doesn't feel right?

LILY. Sara wasn't being stood up in that pub. She was going there after work so that she wouldn't have to go home. Because her boyfriend was violent and…

She'd wait until he'd be asleep. And then go home.

OFFICER. Right.

LILY. So her boyfriend, Sara's boyfriend. Has he been interviewed?

,

,

OFFICER. We asked you for your expertise around ritualistic murder. You gave that to us. It did not shed any further light on the case. We no longer require your help.

LILY. But. You're ignoring the truth.

OFFICER. We did not ask you to investigate the case.

LILY. But you /

OFFICER. You can stop now. It's over.

,

(*Asking because she has to.*) Is there anything else I can help you with?

,

,

LILY. There is actually.

OFFICER. Good. Great. Please, stay awhile.

LILY. You know I mentioned, my friend.

OFFICER. Mmm.

LILY. It's escalated.

OFFICER. Well why isn't she here with you?

LILY. Because. It's escalated. It's dangerous for her. But she's sent me photographic evidence of domestic crimes.

LILY *shows the* OFFICER *her phone.*

OFFICER. Has she given her consent for the photos to be shared?

LILY. She has.

The OFFICER *scrolls through the photos.*

OFFICER. So her claim is that these injuries are connected to her boyfriend?

LILY. Yes.

OFFICER. And she's still absent from work?

LILY. Well, no she doesn't work with me anymore.

A crackly voice from the OFFICER*'s radio: 'Down through the years I have witnessed all sorts of behaviour by these* *officers: including surfing crime reports looking for female victims who live alone…'*

What's that noise?

The OFFICER *tries to turn it off but it doesn't stop.*

Voice on radio continues: '…contacting them via social media when off-duty and offering "support"…'

OFFICER. It's just my radio. There's something wrong with it.

Voice on radio continues: '…talking about intimate details of the crime reports to officers not involved in the investigation.'

The OFFICER *manages to turn off her radio.*

It's stopped now.

LILY. It hasn't stopped. It won't stop.

OFFICER. So. Why doesn't she just leave?

LILY. What?

OFFICER. Your friend. Why doesn't she just leave? If it's that bad.

,

LILY. That's not the right question to ask.

The OFFICER *looks down at the photos again, scrolling through.*

,

OFFICER. I'm going to get these printed.

,

LILY. I thought you were paperless?

OFFICER. Not for case evidence.

The OFFICER *prints the photos.*

It goes into a file.

The OFFICER *files the photos.*

,

LILY. Do you know a police officer – or Sergeant, I think he is – called Dominic De Luca?

The OFFICER *looks at her.*

OFFICER. No.

LILY. You don't?

OFFICER. No, I don't.

,

Thank you for the photographic evidence you provided, Lily. We'll look into it.

,

LILY. Can I have my phone back?

OFFICER. We need to take a quick look at it.

LILY. Why?

OFFICER. It's just protocol.

The OFFICER *puts the phone in an evidence bag.*

It will be easier if you just cooperate.

Love

Back at the flat, DOM *is cleaning the kitchen, giving* ASH *the silent treatment.*

ASH. What's wrong?

Did you not get the promotion?

Did they give it to Trent?

,

Do you want to see what I've packed?

I think I've got way too much.

,

DOM. Did you message anyone?

ASH. What? No.

You can check the phone.

DOM. You've deleted the messages.

ASH. No.

DOM. Do you think I'm fucking stupid? It says 'message deleted'.

,

Did you message Lily?

ASH. No.

He hits her in the face, hard. She falls to the floor.

DOM. Don't fucking lie to my face.

,

,

,

He crouches down to look at ASH, *a bruise rising on her cheek.*

Are you okay?

I didn't mean to.

I'm sorry.

I won't ever do that again.

ASH. Something needs to change, Dom.

DOM. I know –

ASH. It's too deep, it's in your blood.

DOM. I want to change.

ASH. It's rotten from the inside. It's just going to get worse.

DOM. But I love you.

ASH. I know.

They end up holding each other.

,

DOM. Wait.

ASH. What?

DOM. Just. Wait.

He goes away. She waits. She looks over at the door. She could leave right now.

She goes towards the door.

He comes back.

He gets down on one knee. Opens a tiny box.

She gasps.

After ASH*'s initial moment of shock, they both laugh in their familiar way.*

I was going to do this in Morocco, on the beach.

But. Yeah.

Will you?

,

I honestly want nothing else in the entire world but you.

,

ASH. You're an idiot.

DOM. I know.

ASH. You get angry.

DOM. I know.

ASH. Fuck.

DOM. Ash this is the best thing though. I'll be so happy. We'll be so happy.

ASH. You won't be angry anymore?

DOM. I promise. This is all I want.

,

Instead of taking the ring, ASH *closes the ring box.*

ASH. Do it again on the beach.

If we're going to do this, let's do it properly.

She kisses him.

Okay?

DOM. Okay.

,

ASH. There's still a few bits I need. Can you get them?

DOM. Sure.

He writes these down in his phone, quietly repeating them back to her.

ASH. Travel adaptor. Insect repellent. And my face cream. You know, the one I have? But it has to be under one hundred millilitres.

DOM. Okay.

I won't be long.

He goes, locking the door from the outside.

ASH *takes some deep breaths. She looks at her face in the mirror.*

She puts her trainers and a running jacket on. She ties her hair up.

She tries the drawer where Dom keeps her phone – it's locked.

She tries the front door but it's double locked from the outside. She can't get out.

She pleads, muttering under her breath, for a way out.

Outside the window, bees.

She looks over to the window.

She opens it.

Bees, louder.

She quickly closes the window, and sits on the floor, thinking.

Slowly, gently, she opens the window.

The bee swarm enters the flat, loud, curious, urgent.

She puts Pan into the box that Dom first brought him in, whispering to him that it's okay.

ASH *turns back to the window. But it's higher up than before.*

She covers Pan's hutch with a blanket.

ASH. I love you.

She scales the wall, it's difficult.

The window keeps rising.

She finally reaches it and pulls herself up onto the ledge.

She looks down at Pan, far below, whose hutch is glowing red, pulsating.

She leans out the window. It's a long way down.

She leaps through the window.

The bees continue.

Pan, alone, in his hutch.

ACT FOUR

Dead Horse

Dance music, even louder than before.

Club lights, wild and frenetic and multicoloured.

ASH *is in the club. This time it really feels like the last dance – a trance that will take her to somewhere she's never been before.*

LILY *enters.*

LILY. Ash?

ASH *can't hear her.*

Ash!

ASH *continues dancing.*

LILY *grabs* ASH*'s arms,* ASH *gasps, resurfacing. She takes a moment to catch her breath.*

They shout over the pounding music.

ASH. I've missed you!

LILY. What!

ASH. I've missed you!

LILY. Same!

ASH. I've left Dom!

LILY. What!

ASH. I left Dom!

,

With a swarm of bees!

LILY. What!

ASH. It's over!

LILY. Shall we go to the toilets!

ASH. What!

LILY. I can't really hear you! Let's go to the toilets!

LILY *takes* ASH*'s hand and they go to the club toilets.*

The music throbs dull through the wall from the dance floor.

Bright bathroom lights.

LILY *can finally see* ASH.

Your face.

ASH. I don't want to take a photo.

LILY. No I wasn't going to.

Pointless anyway.

ASH. Why?

LILY. They took my phone. Then when they sent the phone back to me, the photos weren't on there and so I called them and they said I had no case number even though I saw them file it. There was a number on the file, anyway, don't worry… you you've left Dom?

ASH. Yeah.

They do that.

They remove the bits they don't want.

I jumped out of the window.

LILY. What?

ASH. But I'm fine. I'm great actually. Do you want a drink?

LILY. Maybe we should just. Make a plan.

ASH. What plan?

LILY. Well what's your plan?

ASH. Dancing. Drinking.

With you?

LILY. But after that.

,

ASH. How come you're here?

LILY. What?

ASH. You don't go out.

LILY. I've been. Coming here.

I like it.

I've been a few times.

ASH. On your own?

,

LILY. (Yeah.) You're on your own.

ASH. Not anymore.

LILY. Maybe we should… do you want to come back to mine?

ASH. Tonight?

LILY. Well where were you planning on staying?

,

ASH. He rescued me.

I don't want you to rescue me. I don't want to keep being rescued.

LILY. I'm not rescuing you. I'm just… here.

LILY *touches* ASH*'s face, gently.*

What happened?

,

,

ASH. I left.

LILY. Ash.

ASH. It's okay.

LILY. It's not okay.

ASH. No it's okay because I have got a plan.

ASH *is smiling now.*

I'm going to do it before he does it.

LILY*'s voice goes weird.*

LILY. Do what?

ASH *is laughing.*

ASH. The bees will do it.

ASH *can't stop laughing.*

He's allergic.

Don't you think that's funny?

LILY. No. Ash please –

ASH. I feel funny.

LILY. What?

ASH. I don't feel good.

ASH *has a seizure.*

LILY. Ash?

ASH. I think you were right.

LILY. What?

ASH. I suck all the bad things towards me. Death of a child. My baby. The fire. Familiar –

Pan! My baby… Seizures. Skin. Marks on my skin. You said it. You were the one who said it.

LILY. Ash… Ash can you hear me?

ASH. I did fuck Charlie and it was Charlie's baby and I asked Dom to hit me, I wanted to feel it.

LILY (*shouting*). Can someone help me please?

ASH. And remember Agnes Godfrey. They said she drowned that horse. They killed her for drowning Mr Webb's horse but it was actually me.

LILY. It's okay. It's okay. I'm going to get someone.

LILY *goes away.*

ASH. Dom?

DOM *appears.*

Didn't you see it?

Dead horse, bleeding and bloated. Floating in the fountain.

DOM. I saw it.

The fountain on the northside of the square. As I was looking at it, I had Nelson's Column in front of me, to the right. And the museum behind me.

ASH. He means the National Gallery.

DOM. Yeah whatever it was, was behind me and…

ASH. He's never been.

It's one of my favourite places and we've never been.

DOM. I pulled her out of a crisis.

ASH. We'll never go now.

DOM. I pulled her out of a cupboard. Tell them.

ASH. He was the officer leading on my domestic abuse case. I was hiding in a cupboard, when he first arrived. So we always have this joke that I'm

ASH *and* DOM. In the closet.

ASH. Maybe I am.

DOM *turns on her but she steps towards him, forcing him backwards, kissing him, an aggressive kiss, more like a dart or a bite.*

Then she laughs.

DOM. I made you laugh.

ASH. Even though my chest was bruised and it hurt to laugh.

DOM. And all the other officers left.

ASH. But you stayed and helped me sweep up the broken glass.

DOM. Dustpan and brush collecting all the tiny pieces.

ASH. And eventually, you were the one who arrested Charlie.

DOM. I saved you.

ASH. Well it was strange actually – because I still loved Charlie and you were so new to me.

DOM. What?

ASH. He hides things, covers things up.

DOM. She struggles a lot with her mental health.

ASH. I've seen inside the horse, amongst the putrefied guts –

DOM. She makes things up.

ASH. All these men. Their skin fusing with the rotting organs –

DOM. I tried to help her but –

ASH. Rotting deeply in the belly of the beast –

DOM. She's lost it.

ASH. I think he might kill me.

DOM. She loves me.

ASH. I imagine it all the time.

DOM. We're engaged.

ASH. I wake up with images of it.

DOM. We're going to Morocco.

ASH. But these bruises perfectly match the size of your thumbs.

She puts his thumb in her mouth.

She bites down hard. Her mouth fills with blood. DOM *cries out.*

Did that hurt?

DOM. It's an offence to assault a police officer.

She spits the blood away.

ASH. But it's not an offence to assault me, is it?

DOM. You need to wake the fuck up.

You're being delusional.

ASH. I'm scared.

DOM. What are you scared of?

ASH. There's a serial killer.

DOM. No there isn't, babe, there's just three women who died.

ASH. There's an epidemic of femicide.

DOM. That's not what epidemic means.

ASH. There's an epidemic of police perpetrated domestic abuse.

DOM. If that was true, it would be on the news.

ASH. Violent men in violent jobs.

DOM. The job makes the men violent.

ASH. An excessive use of force has been reported in hundreds of cases.

DOM. You don't know what I've seen.

ASH. The system doesn't work.

DOM. You don't know the system.

ASH. Yes I do.

There's an epidemic of /

DOM. No one can hear you.

ASH. Why not?

DOM. Because no one cares.

DOM *leaves.*

LILY. Ash!

ASH *wakes from her seizure. The club toilets.*

Can you hear me?

ASH. What?

LILY. There's a medic coming.

ASH. Why?

LILY. You were having a seizure.

ASH. I'm fine.

LILY. You're bleeding.

ASH. I bit my thumb.

LILY. What?

ASH. I bit my tongue.

LILY *dabs the blood away with toilet paper.*

I want to go to the police.

LILY. But he is the police.

ASH. I want to tell someone what's happening. All of it. Right from the beginning. From the inside. Because I know the system. And you know the system.

LILY. I think we should go to the hospital.

ASH. I've got a clear head. I've never had such a clear head.

Someone has to listen.

LILY. It could be big. Really big.

ASH. I know.

But you'll be there. And Pan.

(*Realising something.*) Fuck.

Pan.

LILY. What?

ASH. My baby. I have to go back.

LILY. To the flat??

ASH. I'll just nip back.

LILY. If you go back you'll never get out.

ASH. He's on nights. If I go now, I'll make it before he gets home and then I'll meet you at the station.

LILY. What station?

ASH. The police station, Lily. Keep up.

LILY. You want me to come with you? To report him?

ASH. Yes. Me and you. And Pan. And your notes.

LILY *nods.*

LILY. I think we have to make an appointment.

ASH. You call them. And I'll get Pan.

LILY. Okay.

ASH. I won't be long.

They hug. LILY *does not want to let go.*

Sting

ASH *climbs back in through the window – it's still open from when she left, but at its normal height.*

ASH *goes to Pan's hutch, gets him out. He is unharmed.*

ASH (*sotto*). You're okay! You're okay you're okay.

She feeds him some carrot.

Come on.

She puts Pan in his box, and goes towards the front door to leave.

But then she hears the bee swarm –

– and DOM *falls through the kitchen door, struggling for breath, his face swollen, his chest tight. He tries to speak, signalling to the bathroom.*

DOM. EpiPen.

ASH *doesn't move, in shock.*

Can't. Find. EpiPen.

For an uncomfortably long time, ASH *does nothing, holding Pan, watching* DOM *suffer.*

She seems frozen, almost calm.

Eventually,

ASH (*sotto*). I packed it. It's in your suitcase.

She continues watching as his breathing becomes more constricted.

And then:

She leaves, with Pan, closing the front door behind her.

In the middle of the floor, DOM *is slowly dying.*

We watch.

Lights begin to fade, as DOM*'s life fades.*

And then ASH *comes back in – she can't let him die.*

She puts Pan's box down, goes to the bedroom, opens the suitcase, gets out the EpiPen, comes back.

She kneels over him.

Stay still.

He tries to stay still.

She slams the EpiPen into his thigh, holds it firmly for three seconds, then collapses on top of him, their heavy breathing in sync, together, intimate.

The bee swarm flies out the open window.

The subsequent silence feels like when you turn off an extractor fan. In this new silence, they breathe together for however long it takes to recover.

She shudders with tears.

I'm sorry I'm sorry I'm so sorry.

DOM *is trying desperately to breathe.*

,

,

I have to go now.

DOM *can't speak yet, he just makes sounds.*

DOM. (Again?)

ASH. I'm taking Pan.

DOM. (Where?)

,

ASH. It's over, Dom.

DOM. No.

ASH. I just tried to kill you.

DOM. (But you didn't.) You saved my life.

(Just) stay.

ASH. No.

DOM. We're engaged.

ASH. No. We're not.

DOM. I've got a surprise.

She picks up Pan's carrier and heads to the door.

Skye's coming with us to Morocco.

She goes to open the door.

(*Finally standing up.*) Wait, wait Ash, wait…

I got the promotion.

ASH. –

DOM. I got the / promotion

ASH. You shouldn't be getting promoted.

He stumbles over to the door, blocking her way.

DOM. Why not?

ASH. Because you're… lying and covering things up and you're not safe.

DOM. I'm not safe?

,

ASH. Just let me go.

DOM. You instructed the bees.

ASH. What?

DOM. You instructed the bees to kill me.

ASH. Dom, that's insane.

DOM. So stay. Please.

He locks the door.

It's not over.

Congratulations

LILY *is outside the police station.*

She makes a call.

No answer. She leaves a voice note.

LILY. Hi. I'm here.

So. The good news is that there's an officer available, who seems nice-ish.

The bad news is that they won't let you bring Pan in, so I'll wait outside with him.

How long are you going to be? The appointment is quite short so we don't want to miss our window.

She ends the message and sends it.

She waits.

She calls again.

No answer. She leaves a voice note.

(*Quickly.*) Also. You can stay at mine tonight obviously. Not in my bed, I mean. I'll set up the sofa bed, which is fine, it's Ikea I've barely ever used it. It's also totally fine if you'd rather not, we can call Refuge, I have the number saved. So. Either way.

She ends the message and sends it. She mutters 'stupid message'.

She waits. Longer this time.

More agitated, checks her watch.

She calls again.

No answer. She leaves a voice note.

Hey, if you've changed your mind, that's okay. It's okay. We don't have to do this now. We don't have to do this ever.

You can just. Walk away from it all and… yeah just let me know where you are. I'll swing by and get you in the car and we can…

Just then a car pulls up.

It's DOM. *In uniform, featuring his new Inspector badge. A hint of mania behind his charming façade.*

LILY *stands frozen.*

DOM. Lily! Everything okay?

LILY. –

DOM. We've been meaning to update you on the investigation.

Turns out there was no link.

But it's always worth checking. So thank you.

LILY. Where's Ash?

DOM. Thought she was with you?

She does Tuesdays with you, no?

LILY. No. I've been trying to call her.

DOM. Ah. She threw her phone in the pond.

Which, as I'm sure you've figured out by now, is a very 'Ash' thing to do.

Best way to contact her is by owl – (DOM *expects a laugh that doesn't happen.*)

LILY *scrutinises him with her eyes, noticing a small mark on his shirt… blood?*

LILY. What's that mark? On your shirt.

DOM *looks down, assumes she's looking at his badge.*

DOM (*smiling*). I got a promotion. Today's actually my first shift as Inspector of the unit.

LILY. –

DOM. Most people say congratulations. Or something to that effect.

For a long time, LILY *does not respond.*

But then she steps towards DOM, *close to his face:*

LILY. We will win.

End.

SOPHIE SWITHINBANK

Sophie Swithinbank is a multi-award-winning playwright and screenwriter, based in London. She is the 2023 winner of the Peggy Ramsay/Film4 Award. Sophie's play *Bacon* (Tony Craze Award Winner 2018) ran at Finborough Theatre in 2022, to critical acclaim, winning four Off West End Awards. *Bacon* has been produced across the UK, Europe, Melbourne, New York, Los Angeles and Seoul. *Bacon* is in development for a feature film adaption with Jeva Films.

Sophie's play *Surrender* was produced at the Arcola Theatre, London, before a run at the Edinburgh Festival Fringe, winning the Summerhall Lustrum Award. As part of an attachment at the National Theatre Studio, Sophie developed a new play *Beans*, which won the Sonia Friedman Productions Prize for Best Play in 2024. *Sting* is in development for a TV adaptation with The Lighthouse Film and TV.

A Nick Hern Book

Sting first published in Great Britain as a paperback original in 2026 by Nick Hern Books Limited, The Glasshouse, 49a Goldhawk Road, London, in association with the Young Vic, London

Cover photography by Myah Asha Jeffers; design by Jedly

Designed and typeset by Nick Hern Books, London
Printed in Great Britain by Mimeo Ltd, Huntingdon, Cambridgeshire PE29 6XX

A CIP catalogue record for this book is available from the British Library

ISBN 978 1 83904 520 2

Woodland CARBON
www.woodlandcarbon.co.uk
NICK HERN BOOKS
Printed on Carbon Captured paper

www.nickhernbooks.co.uk/environmental-policy

Nick Hern Books' authorised representative in the EU is
Easy Access System Europe – Mustamäe tee 50, 10621 Tallinn, Estonia
email gpsr.requests@easproject.com

Other Titles in this Series

Waleed Akhtar
THE ART OF ILLUSION *after* Alexis Michalik
KABUL GOES POP: MUSIC TELEVISION AFGHANISTAN
THE P WORD
THE REAL ONES

Jack Bradfield
THE HABITS

Sophia Chetin-Leuner
PORN PLAY
SAVE + QUIT
THIS MIGHT NOT BE IT

Martin Crimp
DEALING WITH CLAIR
THE TREATMENT

Mohamed-Zain Dada
BLUE MIST
DIZZY
SPEED

Phoebe Eclair-Powell
DORIAN *with* Owen Horsley *after* Oscar Wilde
EPIC LOVE AND POP SONGS
FURY
HARM
SHED: EXPLODED VIEW
WINK

Sam Holcroft
COCKROACH
DANCING BEARS
EDGAR & ANNABEL
A MIRROR
PINK
RULES FOR LIVING
THE WARDROBE
WHILE YOU LIE

Branden Jacobs-Jenkins
APPROPRIATE
THE COMEUPPANCE
GLORIA
AN OCTOROON

Lucy Kirkwood
BEAUTY AND THE BEAST *with* Katie Mitchell
BLOODY WIMMIN
THE CHILDREN
CHIMERICA
HEDDA *after* Ibsen
THE HUMAN BODY
IT FELT EMPTY WHEN THE HEART WENT AT FIRST BUT IT IS ALRIGHT NOW
LUCY KIRKWOOD PLAYS: ONE
MOSQUITOES
NSFW
RAPTURE
TINDERBOX
THE WELKIN

Charley Miles
BLACKTHORN
DAUGHTERHOOD
THERE ARE NO BEGINNINGS

Hannah Moscovitch
RED LIKE FRUIT

Chloë Moss
CHRISTMAS IS MILES AWAY
CORRINA, CORRINA
FATAL LIGHT
THE GATEKEEPER
HOW LOVE IS SPELT
RUN SISTER RUN
THIS WIDE NIGHT
THE WAY HOME

Ava Pickett
1536
BLOODSPORT: AFTER HELEN OF TROY
EMMA *after* Jane Austen
THE MANNINGTREE WITCHES *after* A. K. Blakemore

Lucy Roslyn
PENNYROYAL

Sophie Swithinbank
BACON
SURRENDER

Jack Thorne
2ND MAY 1997
AFTER LIFE *after* Hirokazu Kore-eda
BUNNY
BURYING YOUR BROTHER IN THE PAVEMENT
A CHRISTMAS CAROL *after* Dickens
THE END OF HISTORY…
HOPE
JACK THORNE PLAYS: ONE
JACK THORNE PLAYS: TWO
JUNKYARD
LET THE RIGHT ONE IN *after* John Ajvide Lindqvist
THE MOTIVE AND THE CUE
MYDIDAE
THE SOLID LIFE OF SUGAR WATER
STACY & FANNY AND FAGGOT
WHEN WINSTON WENT TO WAR WITH THE WIRELESS
WHEN YOU CURE ME
WOYZECK *after* Büchner

debbie tucker green
BORN BAD
DEBBIE TUCKER GREEN PLAYS: ONE
DIRTY BUTTERFLY
EAR FOR EYE
HANG
NUT
A PROFOUNDLY AFFECTIONATE, PASSIONATE DEVOTION TO SOMEONE (– NOUN)
RANDOM
STONING MARY
TRADE & GENERATIONS
TRUTH AND RECONCILIATION

Jane Upton
ALL THE LITTLE LIGHTS
SCENES FROM A FRIENDSHIP
(THE) WOMAN

Phoebe Waller-Bridge
FLEABAG

www.nickhernbooks.co.uk

@nickhernbooks